STORIES BEHIND
MEN
of
FAITH

Other Books by Ace Collins

Turn Your Radio On: The Stories behind Gospel Music's
    All-Time Greatest Songs
The Cathedrals: The Story of America's
    Best-Loved Gospel Quartet
Stories behind the Best-Loved Songs of Christmas
Stories behind the Hymns That Inspire America
Stories behind the Great Traditions of Christmas
I Saw Him in Your Eyes: Everyday People
    Making Extraordinary Impact
More Stories behind the Best-Loved Songs of Christmas
Stories behind the Traditions and Songs of Easter
Stories behind Women of Extraordinary Faith
Farraday Road

STORIES BEHIND
MEN
of
FAITH

Bestselling Author
ACE COLLINS

ZONDERVAN.com/
AUTHORTRACKER
follow your favorite authors

ZONDERVAN

Stories behind Men of Faith
Copyright © 2009 by Andrew Collins

Requests for information should be addressed to:
Zondervan, *Grand Rapids, Michigan* 49530

ISBN 978-0-310-26317-3

Interior design by Michelle Espinoza

Printed in the United States of America

09 10 11 12 13 14 15 • 21 20 19 18 17 16 15 14 13 12 11 10 9 8 7 6 5 4 3 2 1

To the late Roger Bennett,
whose legacy lives on in the music he created
and the faith he lived each day of his all-too-short life

CONTENTS

INTRODUCTION

As I finished this book, I was struck by how much each of these men have in common with each of us. Marveling at that, I studied what set these sixteen men apart from most churchgoing people I have known in my life. Then as I thought about why these men have such great legacies, I came to a simple conclusion. Let me explain.

I love classic cars. I can spend hours reading about them, working on the ones I have been blessed to own, and enjoying these great automobiles at shows. But for every wonderful example of vintage automotive design that I see on public display, scores of others are hidden from me and everyone else. It is a sad fact that many rare cars are restored but then never used for their intended purpose. In other words, they are never driven. Often when people do remove them from storage, they trailer these mechanical marvels to shows, set them on the ground, surround them with ropes to keep people away, and then reinforce their security efforts by adding signs that say Do Not Touch. A true fan cannot get close enough to really study what made these automobiles true legends of the road. So at most shows these incredible cars are looked at briefly from afar, only to have people quickly move on to spend much more time with the vehicles they can get close to and touch.

As much as this hideaway mentally happens in the world of car restoration, it is even more apparent when I come across people who own fine china and crystal stemware. These items, made for the sole purpose of being a platform for food and a container for liquids, are usually carefully tucked away and saved for those dinners when only the most distinguished guests come to visit. Sadly, in most of the cases I have seen, no guests who enter these homes are ever extraordinary enough to rate bringing out the really good stuff. Therefore it is never used. More often than not, when the fine china and crystal finally make their dramatic appearance on a dining table, it is when these expensive pieces are sold at an estate sale.

Then there are those folks who purchase an outstandingly styled dress or suit. After the purchase, they take a few moments to admire themselves in their bedroom mirror before carefully packing the item away, vowing to bring it out only when there is an event worthy of something this incredible. Thus the outfit never goes to church or to work, and it doesn't make it to local banquets or special programs. In fact, as time marches on, it never sees the light of day but just moves farther and farther back in the closet. If the dress or suit is ever worn at all, it is when the person who bought it is dressed in it for their own funeral.

I have found that too often faith is treated in much the same fashion as classic cars, fine china, and the nicest outfit in the closet. It is trotted out on Sunday morning, as well as sometimes during Christmas and Easter, and then carefully tucked away. It seems to me that for most folks faith is something not to put to work in the real world but to guard and only present on very special and "religious" occasions. And even in those times, faith is rarely seen in actions, words, excitement, or charity. Thus faith seems to have Do Not Touch signs hanging all over it and is stored away with the idea of "saving it for the day that Christ comes to dinner."

While researching and writing this book, I discovered that Christian heroes live their faith each day, displaying it whenever they can and taking it to places others don't dare go. Heroes realize their faith isn't perfect, but that doesn't keep them from putting it out there to show people how much it means to them. Heroes aren't afraid to get a few nicks or chips in their faith, nor are they scared to get their faith a bit dusty. Thus by displaying their faith 24/7, the men highlighted in these pages have inspired millions, led countless souls to follow in their steps, and created legacies that have brought light into a dark world. While the legacies and ways of exhibiting their faith differ vastly from one man to the next, each man has changed the world (or is changing the world) simply by courageously living that faith.

Most important, these men are really not much different from most of us. What sets them apart is that they took their faith out of the closet and into the world. They didn't rope it off and put up Do Not Touch signs, nor did they save it for special guests or special occasions. They presented their faith freely and put it into action everywhere they *lived* their calling. That is how they followed Christ's example and how they changed the world in ways they never imagined.

You will learn that few of these heroes found their calling early—many struggled for decades in search of that calling—but in each case God used these men's life experiences to finally allow them to meet goals they never dreamed possible. So they found, as I hope you will find, that it is never too late to bring the good stuff out of the soul's closet and display it in the real world!

The ultimate question that we must answer is whether we have the courage and conviction to follow their lead. If we do, we too can become heroes of faith.

1

BONO
Putting Faith into Works

Rarely does anyone see Paul Hewson without his dark glasses. He seems to wear them everywhere. They are almost as much a part of his iconic image as his music and charitable causes. In a way, those glasses visually define the Irish rock singer the world knows as Bono. Yet the tinted spectacles are not a stage prop. They serve a real purpose. As the Rock and Roll Hall of Famer told *Rolling Stone* magazine, "I have very sensitive eyes to light. If somebody takes my photograph, I will see the flash for the rest of the day. My right eye swells up. I've a blockage there, so that my eyes go red a lot. So it's part vanity, part privacy, and part sensitivity."

If the eyes are a window to the soul, this entertainment legend's eyes reveal a soul that is in tune with not only the ever-changing world of music but also the rock-solid teachings of Jesus Christ. After all, those same sensitive eyes have allowed Bono to see suffering where millions of others see nothing. Those eyes lead him into worlds and situations others ignore. Through his eyes we see Bono's heart and come to know his passion.

Talent might be the reason he has been nominated for an Academy Award, a Golden Globe, and a Grammy, yet it is his faith that has led Bono to be nominated for the Nobel Peace Prize three times. Most important, it is the singer's putting that faith into action that led *Time* magazine to name Bono one of the one hundred most influential people in the world. The product of the marriage of a Catholic mother and a Protestant father, born in the midst of some of Ireland's bloodiest days of religious and political strife, he seems an unlikely candidate for a worldwide instrument of Christian change, but that has not stopped the short, stocky singer from emerging as a bridge between cultures, faiths, and races. In a world where fame and fortune are the ultimate most men strive for, this Irishman has taken these two rare commodities and made them into something greater—a platform for a calling.

In the mid-nineteenth century, settlers had to traverse the hazardous desert areas of Utah, Arizona, and Nevada on their way to California. As they steered their wagons through the hot, parched sands of the massive Mojave Desert, they noted a tree that somehow thrived in conditions so foreboding that little else survived. These hearty pioneers saw this tree, with its skyward-facing limbs covered in long, dark-green leaves, as a symbol of faith. The tree seemed to be reaching out toward God in hopes of receiving his blessing. Thus it is hardly surprising that the image created by this slow-growing tree reminded many of these weary travelers of the Old Testament hero Joshua.

Almost two centuries later Paul "Bono" Hewson looked upon the same scene. In fact, as Joshua trees often live more than two hundred years, he might have even been seeing the same trees that once grabbed the attention of early American pioneers. Like those who came into this desert before him, the Irishman was struck by the trees' stark beauty, incredible resilience, and undying determination. And like those earlier visitors, he was reminded of something of much greater scope than even the vast wastelands of the western United States. Even as those trees reached toward heaven, Bono felt himself seeking God. He too was reaching up in an effort to find a way to do the Lord's work in his own world.

In the next few weeks after viewing those trees, Bono composed much of what became one of the most important pieces of music in the history of rock. When he and his band, U2, cut *The Joshua Tree*, it not only cemented their place as the world's premier rock band but also built a platform of both fame and fortune that would allow them to speak about a message baptized in faith but only fully realized in works. It was an electric moment when the group's spiritual message merged with their unique sound, yet few then realized what it would mean to millions of poor, sick, dying people all around the globe.

The Joshua Tree marked not the zenith for U2 but just the beginning. However, to fully understand the mighty works built by the music and the work inspired by a tree, one has to go back to 1960 and the place a rock star was born.

Bono's musical masterpiece was created from almost three decades of life experiences. Raised just outside of Dublin, the future star was the second child of Bobby and Iris Hewson. Those who knew the active youngster often referred to him as an "exasperating child." He possessed boundless energy, infinite curiosity, and a great desire to learn. He questioned everything—demanding answers on subjects ranging from the color of the sky to biblical history—while also constantly finding new ways to get into trouble. Upbeat by nature, he nevertheless saw pain and suffering and considered the cost of both. Even as a child, he noted the poverty and despair when traveling through the Dublin slums and wondered what could be done to change the fortunes of these poor people. It seemed that when people hurt, so did he.

A part of this sensitivity to suffering could probably be traced to his parents. Though they came from vastly different backgrounds and seemingly very dissimilar perspectives, they easily presented their faith in words as well as actions. Yet even as Paul embraced the Christ his parents called Lord, he noted the irony of the religious war that split Ireland's Catholics and Protestants and kept his parents from worshiping their common God in the same church.

"I remember how my mother would bring us to chapel on Sundays while my father used to wait outside," he explained. "One of the things that I picked up from my father and my mother was the sense that religion often gets in the way of God."

This unique viewpoint would ultimately drive the young man away from organized Christianity and push him to something that put wings to his prayers—going beyond the ways of the church to do the ways of the Lord. Yet a transformation like that could not happen without power. And like most teens in the early 1970s, Paul was powerless to act on his vision. However, the fact that he noted the central irony of his parents' faith—brought together by Christ and separated by man—showed a depth of understanding that set him apart from his peers and would lead to him someday changing the perspectives of millions.

To say that the youngest Hewsen was a different sort of lad was stating the obvious. Though he could be tough when standing up for what he believed, he seemed to have been born with the soul of an artist. While others ran in fear from honeybees, he was known to lift them from hives, speak to them as they perched on his fingers, then set them back down on their homes. He was just as kind and gentle to senior citizens, as well as to kids who didn't seem to fit with their peers. Although he was talented, intelligent, and creative, it would take a tragedy to add two other essential elements to those gifts—focus and drive.

At the age of fifteen, Paul was attending his grandfather's funeral when his mother died of a brain aneurysm. He was devastated. Seeking an outlet for his grief, he turned to music. Listening to the top rock acts of the day inspired the boy to focus on playing the guitar and developing his vocal skills. After all, starting with Elvis, that was how young men gained the spotlight that paved the way to fame and fortune.

Not content to play alone, Paul responded to a notice on a bulletin board. Another high school student, Larry Mullen, wanted to start a band and had advertised to attract a few like-minded kids to an open audition. Guitarist Dave Evans, who was known as The Edge, and bass player Adam Clayton also showed up with their instruments. At the time, Mullen was the best of the lot, and

Paul was no doubt the worst. At that first rehearsal what gained Paul a spot in the group was more his poetic skills and his rather theatrical personality than his music. Even when he was bad and had problems carrying a tune, he was still bigger than life when he picked up a microphone.

Like thousands of other high school bands, the group would have probably gone nowhere if the four had not all been students at the progressive Mount Temple Comprehensive School in Clontarf. The school's headmaster, John Brooks, encouraged thinking, discussing ideas, and debating. When kids told him they didn't like the way a class was conducted or a schedule made up, Brooks challenged them to present a better way. A driven, Christian man, Brooks wanted his students to not just live a faithful life but be spurred into action. He seemed to believe his students could fix the ancient religious strife in Ireland if they would get beyond labels and put their faith to work.

When Brooks learned of a new rock group being formed by some of his most unique students, he saw it as a sure way to keep the kids off the streets and out of trouble as well as give voice to a new generation's ideas. With the help of a teacher he trusted, Brooks encouraged the quartet, even allowing them to use the school auditorium on weeknights and weekends for rehearsals. Brooks's giving them access to this venue provided the fledgling rockers with the hours they needed to hone their skills. It was during this time of maturation that Paul, who had already gone through several nicknames, including Steinvic von Huyseman, Houseman, and Bon Murray, became Bonovox of O'Connell Street. *Bonovox*, a Latin word for "a man with a good voice," was a tribute to Paul's growth as a singer. Over time the *vox* was dropped, and the boy was known to his classmates as simply Bono.

In addition to his work in the band, which first played at local church-sponsored gatherings, Bono was a solid student who loved history. Yet it would not be his grades or his knowledge of the past that took the young man out of the Dublin suburbs to meetings with presidents and popes; it would be his group, U2.

In the mid-1970s, Dublin was an ethnic and cultural melting pot. Not only was Irish history found in this ancient city, but a wide range of peoples from all over the world now lived in the area. This mix of old and new created an Ireland that blended everything from American TV to British rock music to local theater. Into this mix came Bono, whose writing style included all these elements plus a deep thirst to create music with a message. Yet at this point the sound U2 was producing was hardly revolutionary. In fact, as the band played clubs in Dublin and later in London, the only thing that set them apart was the lead singer's dynamic charisma. He had the Elvis factor that drew people toward the stage even when what he was singing didn't stick in their minds. This showmanship paved the way for CBS Records to take a chance on signing U2 to a recording contract.

In 1980 the band had a single that saw moderate success, but their album failed to generate much in the way of sales. Unable to create enthusiasm in London, U2 faced a bleak future. Then the group was booked on a tour of the United States. This American experience put the band on the map. A tribute to Dr. Martin Luther King Jr., "Pride (In the Name of Love)" marked their first chart success in 1984, but it was U2's dynamic stage performances that really built their reputation. They seemed to possess a joy in performing that few other groups could match. U2 lifted the audience to a higher plane, while many others often left their fans in a blue funk. Americans related to it in a unique way that had been missed in the UK. So while they were little more than another band in their hometown, they were seen as innovative superstars in the United States.

As fans latched on to U2, Bono embraced America, completely entranced by the country's great contrasts. He marveled at the huge cities, the diverse culture, and the wide-open spaces filled with breathtaking natural beauty. Yet he was also shocked by the USA's violence, poverty, and appalling waste of God-given resources. He sensed the nation had dynamic potential but wondered if it was dying spiritually. It was a place that wanted so desperately to be seen as Christian, while at the same time many of its people seemed to try to run from that label. Yet rock's latest and largest icon was not running from it. During a period when other rockers embraced all kinds of New Age themes, he told both the press and his fans, "One other thing you should know ... we're all Christians."

Many thought Bono's claim might spell an end to the band's success in mainstream rock, yet while this religious admission might have been front-page news for other groups, it was largely ignored in the case of U2. Hence, for the moment, the message the singer wanted people to hear was generally lost as well.

Seemingly overnight U2 became hot, and as his group toured the globe, Bono's sensitive eyes were opened to a plethora of conditions he had never fully comprehended. The poverty he saw in many places sickened him. As money and fame rolled in, a time when he should have been on top of the world, his heart grew heavy. He found himself with more questions than answers. Why was he being blessed when so many were starving to death? Why was he on the cover of *Time* and *Rolling Stone* when millions of dying babies were being ignored? Where were the world's priorities?

The men who made up U2 all read the Bible. The members often discussed certain elements of the Gospels and how they related to what they observed in their travels. Many times they asked what Christ would have thought of the world they saw each day. In fact, when *Rolling Stone* questioned Bono if U2 was a revolutionary band, he replied, "If sitting in the back of our bus and reading the Bible makes us revolutionary, then I guess we are."

He told writer John Waters, "Judeo Christianity is about the idea that God *is* interested in you.... This was a radical thought: that God who created the universe might be interested in me.... It is the most extraordinary thought."

Yet sitting and reading the Bible, knowing God loved him, being blessed more than he could imagine, and being worshiped as a rock idol onstage were simply not enough for the singer. Bono honestly felt that being blessed meant that he needed to bless others. Thus in 1985, when Bob Geldof organized the Live Aid concerts, U2 was one of the first to jump on board. Bono and the group were thrilled to have the opportunity to play in a concert where all the money would go to feeding starving people in Africa. As the world tuned in, scores of the globe's greatest acts took to the stage and raised more than $200 million to fight the famine. Yet after the televised concerts in England and the United States ended, almost all the entertainers went back to their mansions congratulating themselves on their splendid act of charity. One did not. For Bono, singing was not enough; he had to do more. What he did would complete his transformation from a man who spoke and wrote about faith to a person who boldly lived his beliefs.

After his Live Aid performance at Wembley Stadium, Bono and his wife, Ali, caught a plane to the region of Africa hardest hit by famine. The couple spent the next six weeks quietly working in an orphanage in Wello, Ethiopia. What he saw as he watched children die in his arms overwhelmed him. Live Aid was not enough. Bono had to wake up the world to the plight of millions of poor people. He saw this blight as a crime against humanity and God. He would not accept that so many had to die because of corruption, neglect, and indifference. It was time someone put the spotlight on these hard-to-stomach facts. Who better to do that than a person whom the spotlight followed everywhere he went.

Bono could have gone to a large church to make his statement, but he felt that affiliating his calling with any one Christian group would limit the work that could be done. What he did had to be nondenominational; otherwise it would become like his early church experience: people left on the outside looking in while others worshiped according to rules written by man.

Bono was consumed by this kind of vision when he stood in the American desert and looked at the Joshua tree. Seized by a passion that flowed from his writing into every facet of his life, he knew it was time to create his masterpiece. Little did he realize how God's hand in this work would change his life as he dramatically changed the world.

Like the man himself, Bono's songwriting had matured. He was now trying to impart something that went beyond the norms for the rock genre but didn't quite cross over into Christian music. The spiritual message was subtle, but through carefully crafted lyrics featuring incredible emotional insights, the musical parables were there for those who wanted to hear them.

The Joshua Tree was something incredibly different for rock music. The album had a big sound with lyrics that embraced huge and complex ideas. In words that reflected on everything from love to the human condition, this amazing work revealed the writer's soul. There were no hooks or gimmicks here, simply Bono at his rawest. As fans listened, they not only enjoyed the music; they thought about what he was trying to say.

With Live Aid behind him, the little guy with the big voice and now even bigger ideas convinced his bandmates that a homecoming concert in Ireland could be used for something greater. Thus even though it was not announced to the press, all the proceeds from the event were given to charity. This was just the seed money for what the singer wanted to accomplish through a combination of his faith and fame. It was simply the start of a long list of good works.

As the power and success of *The Joshua Tree* was making it the most important album of the era, U2's talkative singer was speaking of his trips to third world countries more than he was speaking of his music. It was clear in the way he spoke that he did so not to bring praise for his efforts for the poor but to try to put the focus on hungry, dying people who needed help. With this unique message of concern, almost always couched in biblical analogies, Bono grew from just another rock star into a man who had something to say and demanded to be heard.

As people listened to his message, they began to question where Bono had learned this philosophy. When asked to flesh out his reasons for reaching out to the poorest of the poor, the rock star spoke of the Sermon on the Mount, the directives of Paul, the parables of Christ, and the wisdom of David. Even though his message embraced faith, he shied away from setting himself up as a Christian role model. When others attempted to frame his work in this context, the modest man pointed to his own shortcomings. He explained that he was far from a saint and nothing like a preacher. Yet even as he begged off the title of Christian leader, he continued to mention tithing and compassion. No rock singer had ever spoken this way before, and yet rather than driving people away from U2's music, this declaration of faith seemed to draw even more fans to the group.

In a move that seems completely foreign to rock, Bono began to read Psalm 116 before singing "Where the Streets Have No Name." He surely realized as he read the Scripture that it was the first time many in the audience had ever heard something from the book of Psalms. He also had to know that some might go home, find a Bible, and start reading it for themselves. A few might just find God and faith in the process. So the man who constantly claimed he wasn't a preacher had somehow found a missionary's voice.

Now sure of his calling, more and more Bono combined biblical statements with modern realities as he pointed out at the National Prayer Breakfast and many other public forums, "It's not a coincidence that in the Scriptures, poverty is mentioned more than 2,100 times. It is not an accident. That's a lot of airtime, 2,100 mentions."

He began to use the attention draped on him by the press to emphasize the need to make a statement. He explained that seeking the Lord's blessing was not enough. He felt it was time to get involved in what God was doing because it had already been blessed.

"You know, the only time Christ is judgmental is on the subject of the poor. 'As you have done it unto the least of these my brethen, you have done it unto me,' Matthew 24:40. As I say, good news to the poor."

In 2005 Bono told *Rolling Stone*, "I believe there's a force of love and logic ... behind the universe. And I believe in the poetic genius of a creator who would choose to express such unfathomable power as a child born in 'straw poverty.' The story of Christ makes sense to me."

As his voice and influence continued to grow, Bono even more fully embraced faith and more often quoted the Bible but still did not align with the organized church. When asked why he could speak so clearly of God's love and not be part of a fellowship of believers, he explained that it was the lukewarm believers who drove him out of church. Bono didn't want a cold passion; what he needed was a church excited enough about God to get their members involved in using their money and putting legs to their faith. That is what he saw God demanding of him. That is how he read Jesus' words to all believers. So he expected no less from every Christian church.

By 2000 Bono's charity work was touching millions. He was giving away much of his own fortune as well. Yet more than that, he was seemingly everywhere there were poor people. He wasn't just viewing the problems; he was getting his hands dirty through actual work. He then returned to the concert trails to expose what he saw.

Bono's example of putting his faith in action brought invitations to speak with everyone from Bill Clinton to George W. Bush. The fact that Pope John Paul II and noted evangelical Protestant icon Dr. Billy Graham both scheduled meetings with him clearly showed that Bono had built a bridge across denominational splits that had once separated worship opportunities for his own parents.

He told those great Christian leaders, as well as thousands of others in a host of different interviews with both print and video media, "I cannot escape my conviction that God is interested in the progress of mankind, individually and collectively." His statement confronted two areas most Europeans and Americans avoided—religion and politics.

HIV/AIDS soon became part of Bono's public outreach. He compared the disease to the leprosy of Christ's era. He pointed to how Jesus had met this earlier problem head-on and how, thanks in large part to Christian concerns and actions, leprosy had been all but eliminated. He demanded that this same kind of action be taken today with AIDS. He pointed out that tens of millions of children were losing their parents to the disease and asked who was going to care for those children. He argued that Christians had to step forward and become their brother's keeper. Bono's powerful message was cited as one of the reasons why the United States dramatically increased foreign aid to Africa.

In a move that shocked many conservative Christians, Bono was asked to speak at the National Prayer Breakfast at the White House in 2006. Dressed in his customary black attire, wearing his glasses and earrings, the rocker challenged politicians, visiting pastors, and laypeople in ways no other speaker at the event had ever done. He held a mirror up and forced them to look at their lack of action. He also presented a window to a world that few wanted to see, but how they listened!

In part of his prepared statement he said, "I was amazed when I first got to America and I learned how much some churchgoers tithe. Some tithe up to ten percent of the family budget. Well, how does that compare with the federal budget, [which is] the budget for the entire American family? How much of that goes to the poorest people of the world? Less than one percent."

At the White House in 2006 he added, "I would suggest to you today that you see the flow of effective foreign assistance as tithing.... Which, to be truly meaningful, will mean an additional one percent of the federal budget tithed to the poor."

After the meeting, President Bush, who had many of his own policies challenged by the singer, said, "He's a doer. The thing about this good citizen of the world is he's used his position to get things done."

Another convert, Richard Cizik of the National Association of Evangelicals, added after the Prayer Breakfast of 2006, "He's ready to be used by God in whatever ways he can, and if we were all so willing, the world would be a better place."

A rock star showing the light to presidents and preachers! Who would have thought it possible? Probably only a man like Bono, who had the vision to see things as Christ saw them.

Today, using his Christian faith as a foundation, Bono openly criticizes governments for not spending more on foreign aid. He points out that for a few dollars, villages in Africa can be saved. For the lack of those dollars, thousands die needlessly each year. He continually makes the statement, "Why should where you live determine whether you live?" His direct words get to the heart of a message many Christians had either forgotten or ignored for generations.

As he told President Bush, "God will not accept that [ignoring the plight of the poor in Africa]. Mine won't, at least. Will yours?" It is a challenge few want to hear, but Bono regularly issues it anyway. And when regular churches begin to see this as their cause, there is little doubt he and millions of others will again be excited by organized Christianity.

For the moment, the rocker is content to continue on a solitary mission of hope and faith. He points out in his speeches on African poverty, "We have the cash, we have the drugs, we have the science, but do we have the will to make poverty history?" And to emphasize the answer to that question, he has put his money where his mouth is.

Many have felt that Bono has done enough. His work and his words have mobilized thousands of people and raised millions of dollars for those he calls "the least of these." Yet when asked when he will quit traveling hundreds of thousands of miles and giving up almost all his free time to what he sees as the cause of Christ, he often cites what could be his motto: "You don't quit halfway up Mt. Everest." Therefore he keeps reading the Bible, studying the world's greatest problems, and praying over both of those things.

When he was asked what made U2 so successful, Bono told *Rolling Stone*, "All you need is three chords and the truth to succeed in rock and roll." Perhaps all you need to do mighty works of faith might be something just as simple—a great message boldly wrapped in biblical truth. How powerful can that message be? Can one man of faith speaking Jesus' words really change the direction and attitudes of people and governments?

When trying to explain the burdens placed on the backs of so many African nations, Bono, speaking at the White House in 2006, gave an American president and many other world leaders this simple statement: "On so many issues it's difficult to know what God wants from us, but on this issue, helping the desperately poor, we know God will bless it."

Thanks to Bono's words and influence, many of the world's richest nations have agreed to cancel the debt of the eighteen poorest African countries. This means that monies once used to pay interest on millions of dollars of loans can now feed millions of starving people. Few things have ever showed the power of faith like this one act of governmental forgiveness.

As a teenager, Bono dreamed of becoming a rock star. Yet his vision took him so far beyond that initial dream. He recently wrote in the book *On the Move*, "God is in the slums, in the cardboard boxes where the poor play house. God is in the silence of a mother who had infected her child with a virus that will end both their lives. God is in the cries heard under the rubble of war. God is in the debris of wasted opportunity and lives, and God is with us if we are with them."

Bono is with the poor, and his prayer is that Christians everywhere join him in living out Matthew 25:34–40. By using his sensitive eyes, he has had the vision to see where God is, and he has had the faith to join the Lord in those tough places. Bono's faith has changed the world, and he wants others to join his band of faith and action. He honestly believes that like U2, you too, if you have the faith, can make an impact on the world.

2

JOHN NEWTON
Breaking the Chains

On Thursday, December 31, 1772, John Newton was working on the message he planned to present to his Olney, England, congregation on New Year's Day. To put himself in the right frame of mind for the special service, the Anglican priest looked back before trying to gauge what lay ahead in 1773. As he took stock of his fifty-two years on earth, he was awed by all that had transpired in his life. He had once been a hopelessly lost soul, an unapologetic wretch who represented the worst of humanity, but now he had a dynamic ministry, a loving and devoted wife, and a church that had embraced him as a father for almost a dozen years. As he inventoried these and so many more amazing blessings, he could not help but mouth, "Praise God."

Overcome with thanks, Newton reached for his journal. Turning to the first empty page, he quickly scribbled, "How many scenes I have passed through in that time! By what a way the Lord has led me! What wonders has He shown me! My book is now nearly full, and I shall provide another for the next year! O Lord, accept my praise for all that is past. Enable me to trust Thee for all that is to come, and give a blessing to all who may read records of Thy goodness and my own vileness. Amen and amen."

Setting his journal to one side, Newton opened his well-worn Bible. It is hardly surprising that the clergyman automatically turned to passages centering on the life of a historic king. Of all those whose stories are detailed in God's Word, Newton most identified with David. At times he felt as if he were the modern recreation of that great but flawed hero of faith.

The preacher freely admitted that he had once been the greatest of sinners. Hence Newton was deeply comforted by the story of David. It proved to him that God could use a man with more faults than could be counted. Both of these men, separated by thousands of years, had sinned terribly; then they had not only found forgiveness but also been used by the Lord in very special ways.

Newton turned to 1 Chronicles 17:16 and read, "Who am I, O LORD God, and what is mine house, that thou hast brought me hitherto?" How far indeed had the Lord brought Newton! Yet there was still a long road to travel and so much more he needed to atone for before his journey was complete. Even after living in the light for half his life, Newton was still very much aware of his dark sins. They haunted his sleep. He was forgiven, but what he had once done was hardly forgotten.

Though Newton was hardly a great orator, his words had been the foundation that had built the Olney church into one of the most dynamic in all of England. Because of the pastor's buoyant message, the church pews were always full, and people hung on his every word. Even a recent major building project had not created enough room for those who came each week to hear the gentle man's message of hope and compassion. While others preached hellfire and damnation, Newton spoke of love and grace. After all, these two powerful divine gifts had saved him, and he knew they would lead others out of the darkness as well.

At the heart of most of his sermons were stories of Newton's own battles with sin. He used examples of his own pre-salvation experiences to highlight the power of God to lift a man out of hell and into the light. Week in and week out he used the word *grace* in letters and sermons as he tried to explain God's greatest and most amazing gift.

As he set aside his Bible, Newton glanced over to a stack of hymns he had recently written with William Cowper. Cowper was a genius, a man who could compose lyrics that resonated stronger than any sermon the preacher had ever penned. His songs, such as "Light Shining out of the Darkness," were dynamic in their scope and power, and hundreds of people had been saved simply by hearing the Lord's call in Cowper's words. Yet the grace he wrote about was lost on the man. The songwriter was deeply troubled, often spiraling into the depths of depression, constantly moaning in spiritual pain and crying for hours on end.

A few days before, Cowper had tried and failed to end his life. This attempt was another in a long line of failed suicide attempts. Now living with Newton and his wife, the songwriter spent as much time pleading for death as he did trying to fight for life. The spiritual battle being waged over the talented man's soul was one of the few negative elements in Newton's world. He simply could not understand how his friend could write so brilliantly about the light but not see it in his own world. If only he could find a way to present the story of grace in a fashion that would touch Cowper's heart and mind. The pastor attempted to tailor a message that would bring peace to the distressed man. In truth, Cowper could not fathom the depth of Newton's words, but the message found on that New Year's Eve would resonate with hundreds of millions in a way nothing ever had.

Picking up a pen, Newton focused on what had become a familiar theme and direction for his sermons. First he told a homespun parable of the fall from grace and redemption.

"A company of travelers fall into a pit: one of them gets a passenger to draw him out. Now he should not be angry with the rest for falling in; nor because they are not yet out, as he is. He did not pull himself out: instead, therefore, of reproaching them, he should shew them pity.... A man, truly illuminated, will no more despise others, than Bartimeus, after his own eyes were opened, would take a stick, and beat every blind man he met."

Rereading his words, Newton wondered if Cowper or others would see themselves in the pit. Would anyone feel the need to accept God's love and be pulled from his or her lowly state? Would this story provide the insight a lost soul needed to accept Christ and walk in faith?

After he finished his text, the clergyman reviewed his sermon, only to discover that while his message of salvation was strong, it was still missing something. Newton glanced back over the songs he had been writing with Cowper, then pulled out a piece of blank paper. Using his own redemptive experience, he carefully crafted lyrics that reflected his message for the January 1 service.

Amazing grace! (how sweet the sound)
That sav'd a wretch like me!
I once was lost, but now am found,
Was blind, but now I see.

'Twas grace that taught my heart to fear,
And grace my fears reliev'd;
How precious did that grace appear,
The hour I first believ'd!

Thro' many dangers, toils and snares,
I have already come;
'Tis grace has brought me safe thus far,
And grace will lead me home.

The Lord has promis'd good to me,
His word my hope secures;
He will my shield and portion be,
As long as life endures.

Yes, when this flesh and heart shall fail,
And mortal life shall cease;
I shall possess, within the veil,
A life of joy and peace.

The earth shall soon dissolve like snow,
The sun forbear to shine;
But God, who call'd me here below,
Will be forever mine.

The last thing he needed was a tune to guide his lyrics on their spiritual ride. Legend has it that the music which first came into his head on that New Year's Eve was an old African melody he had once heard while serving on a slave ship. As Newton was using much of his own personal testimony in the verses of his hymn, it would have been logical for him to remember the haunting strains of a chained man singing in the bowels of the ship. After all, the pain that Newton had helped create for thousands like that man was as much a part of who he was as the church he now served. This was the pre-grace Newton, and as he once more looked back over his life, it was amazing that this despicable human being had ever found God's grace.

Newton was born in London on July 24, 1725. From the beginning, his life was a study in contrasts. His mother was a devout Christian who set aside time for daily devotionals. A gentle woman, she filled her son with stories of Moses, David, and Jesus and taught him many of the hymns penned by Isaac Watts. She told him that the most powerful force on earth was not the British navy but the Lord's grace. She constantly prayed that her words and actions would set the boy on the right course.

Yet these lessons were often muted by the drunken ravings of the boy's father, a hard-living sailor who felt that compassion was a sign of weakness and that prayers were the practice of fools. He wanted his boy to follow in his footsteps, to be the toughest man on the seas, and to embrace a life of sinful lusts that knew no bounds.

This war for a son's soul might have played out much differently if Elizabeth Newton had lived. Sadly, the lad was just six when he stood by his mother's grave and said goodbye for the final time. A few days later John Newton Sr. returned to the sea, leaving the younger John to pretty much fend for himself. During this period the boy rarely went to school; he spent many of his days involved in petty crimes. By the age of ten he was running with street gangs and could outdrink, outcuss, and outfight many grown men. These almost demonic traits impressed his father enough to take the boy with him to sea. By his eighteenth birthday Newton had sailed the Mediterranean five times and carried the scars of countless barroom brawls.

The sea fascinated Newton. Both beautiful and menacing, it could be calm at one moment or powerful and dangerous the next. Thus sailing was both unpredictable and intoxicating. He might have grown to love it if not for his relationship with his father. The elder Newton assaulted the lad with both words and fists. Newton would later write of the relationship, "I was with him in a state of fear and bondage. His sternness ... broke and overawed my spirit."

In an attempt to break free from the chains of his abusive father, Newton jumped ship, hoping to find work on solid ground. During his short days ashore, he met a beautiful young woman, but before he could form a lasting relationship, he was captured and taken back to sea duty, this time as a midshipman on the *Harwich*.

By now the mold had been cast. John was his father's son, constantly fighting and struggling against those in command, hurling fists and insults whenever he gained the opportunity. He often deserted during shore leaves only to be caught, whipped, and placed in chains belowdecks. Yet even after being stripped naked and publicly beaten, he did not back down. He still hurled epithets and spit on anyone who dared cross him. Over time his behavior became so irrational and his rage so deep that many of the hardened crewmen felt Newton was possessed. It seemed the only time he showed any signs of peacefulness was when he was passed out drunk.

Finally, when Newton was twenty, the officers of the *Harwich* gave up on him and left him on a small island off the coast of Sierra Leone, West Africa. In short order he was captured by a local farmer, who treated him more like an animal than a human being. Newton often toiled sixteen hours a day and was given a single meal when tossed into his cell-like quarters at night. He probably would have died if not for the slaves who smuggled him food. Kept in bondage, he was barely alive when a ship's captain bought him from the farmer a year and a half later.

Overjoyed to be off the island, Newton settled into a life as a seaman on a slave trader. He worked alongside men who were truly his peers. Those Newton now called brothers were the sickest of the sick, the vilest of the vile, and the most depraved men on the earth. Newton joyfully bragged that he was the worst of the lot. Like him, these despicable sailors had been kicked off respectable ships so many times that now the only ones willing to employ them were those hauling human cargo.

In that day the slave ships sailed in unchanging pattern. They left England with little cargo, going south to the African coast. Once there, the men who had the reputation as the best barterers would take a longboat to shore and meet with local chiefs. These tribal leaders would look through a few trunks filled with weapons, ammunition, liquor, clothing, cheap jewelry, and food. After several hours of negotiations, a deal would be made, and the slave traders would be escorted to an area where scores of men and women were held captive. The strongest of these captives would then be culled from this group and put in chains. Once on the ship, they were taken belowdecks, forced to lie down, then strapped down like bags of grain. One row of human flesh was followed by another and another until six hundred souls were tied down in the unventilated confines of the wooden vessel.

For the next several weeks the slave trader would race across the Atlantic at full sail, desperate to make record time, as every extra day meant more of the cargo would die en route. When the frightened Africans gave way to heat or disease, they were picked up and tossed over the side. No words were spoken, no prayers were said, and no tears were shed. Newton threw men and women into the sea as casually as he would have pitched a bag of garbage. The cries and moans that came from below the deck meant nothing to him. After a while he grew so callous and cold he didn't even hear them.

In America the fresh crop of black slaves was traded for goods such as sugar, corn, and cotton. Then the triangle was completed with a trip back to England to finally trade the goods from the New World for British pounds. For more than a century, slave trading was one of the most profitable ventures in the world. For men like Newton, their cut provided enough pocket change to purchase all the pleasure they could want in the ports where their ships stopped.

In 1748 Newton and the crew of the *Greyhound* had traded another batch of human cargo for a shipful of precious goods. After months at sea, moods were high. As the seamen drank rum and ate fresh food from America, they considered what they would do with the bounty that awaited them once the journey was complete. Their ultimate goal was to live out the old English creed of "eat, drink, and be merry."

Tiring of the games of chance and stories of adventure, Newton left the deck for his quarters. Once below, he found a book, *Imitation of Christ*. Written by Thomas à Kempis in 1418, the book presented a formula for Christian living. This was hardly something that would have seemed to appeal to the hardened Newton. Perhaps he had decided to read it because of memories of his mother's faith, but more than likely he had picked it up simply because there were so few reading choices aboard the *Greyhound*. He was about halfway through the book when he put it down and drifted off to sleep.

A few hours later Newton was awakened by a sudden violent rocking. As he quickly discovered, March 10, 1748, was to be a night he would never forget. His vessel was under siege, not by an enemy of the British Empire but by a massive storm. Swinging from his bed, he found himself knee-deep in water. Racing toward the deck, he heard the captain cry out for a knife. "You get it," the man in front of him snarled as he tossed himself upward. A second later that sailor was washed into the raging sea. As he watched the man sink under the angry waves, Newton was fully aware that he was likely to die on this very night. Considering the words in the book he had been reading, he fell to his knees in the water and screamed out, "If this will not do, the Lord have mercy upon us." It was the first sincere prayer he had offered since his mother's death.

Newton spent hours at the ship's pumps, trying to stay ahead of the water falling from the sky and leaping over the deck into the ship. All around him men were crying out for mercy. The same sailors who just hours before had bragged about their sins were now asking God for his help. Yet their pleas seemed unheard as the storm's gales pushed the boat like a feather in the wind. Exhausted, the captain asked Newton to take over the helm. Tying himself in place, the strong seaman fought the storm. The war he waged would continue into the morning and through the next afternoon. Finally, almost twenty hours after it had begun, the hurricane passed. Years later Newton wrote about that moment, "I thought I saw the hand of God displayed in our favour. I began to pray."

Yet even after this harrowing experience, Newton could not admit his own sins. He could not even confess that he was not in control of his own life. Instead he offered thanks but little more. A day later he found a Bible and happened upon Luke 11:13: "If ye then, being evil, know how to give good gifts unto your children: how much more shall your heavenly Father give the Holy Spirit to them that ask him?"

Though he didn't make a profession of faith, he did admit, "If this book be true, the promise in this passage must be true likewise. I have need of that very Spirit, by which the whole was written, in order to understand it aright. He has engaged here to give that Spirit to those who ask: I must therefore pray for it; and, if it be of God, he will make good on his own word."

The *Greyhound* would make landfall in Ireland on April 8. During the time from the storm to that day, Newton kept to himself while considering both his faith and his fate. As he saw the green shores, he felt cleansed. "I stood in need of an Almighty Savior; and such a one I found described in the New Testament. Thus far the Lord had wrought a marvelous thing: I was no longer an infidel: I heartily renounced my former profaneness, and had taken up some right notions; was seriously disposed, and sincerely touched with a sense of the undeserved mercy I had received, in being brought safe through so many dangers. I was sorry for my past misspent life, and purposed an immediate reformation. I was quite freed from the habit of swearing, which seemed to have been as deeply rooted in me as a second nature. Thus, to all appearance, I was a new man."

His fellow crewmen were amazed at the transformation. Newton didn't want to go to the pub and get drunk, he was suddenly respectful to those around him, and he was no longer cursing. Yet as he was later to confess, the change was really only skin-deep. "I acknowledged the Lord's mercy in pardoning what was past, but depended chiefly upon my own resolution to do better for the time to come." In other words, he still felt he was master of his own spirit and life.

A few months later he was remaining true to his vow of refraining from drinking or cursing but had no problem accepting the captaincy of a slave trader and setting sail for the African coast. He would write in his journal, "With our ships, the great object is to be full. When the ship is there, it is thought desirable she should take as many as possible. The cargo of a vessel of a hundred tons, or little more, is calculated to purchase from two hundred and twenty to two hundred and fifty slaves. Their lodging-rooms below the deck, which are three (for the men, the boys, and the women), besides a place for the sick, are sometimes more than five feet high, and sometimes less; and this height is divided towards the middle, for the slaves lie in two rows, one above the other, on each side of the ship, close to each other, like books upon a shelf. I have known them so close that the shelf would not, easily, contain one more. And I have known a white man sent down, among the men, to lay them in these rows to the greatest advantage, so that as little space as possible might be lost.

"Let it be observed, that the poor creatures, thus cramped for want of room, are likewise in irons, for the most part both hands and feet, and two together, which makes it difficult for them to turn or move, to attempt either to rise or to lie down, without hurting themselves, or each other. Nor is the motion of the ship, especially her heeling, or stoop on one side, when under sail, to be omitted; for this, as they lie athwart, or cross the ship, adds to the uncomfortableness of their lodging, especially to those who lie on the leeward or leaning side of the vessel."

As he bargained for these captives, as he watched many of them die and be tossed into the sea, as he heard their moans and even observed them sold as common cargo, the supposedly redeemed Newton felt no remorse. For six years, even after his marriage on February 1, 1750, he continued to make the triangle, carrying thousands of Africans away from their home and thinking nothing of seeing them treated like livestock or dying along the way.

"During the time I was engaged in the slave trade, I never had the least scruple as to its lawfulness." He also did not consider its morality or the fact that those he stacked into the ship's hold had souls that were just as important to God as his own.

There can be little doubt that Newton would have continued to bargain in human souls if he had not been brought to his knees by a sudden epileptic seizure in 1754. He was preparing to leave for Africa when a pain shot through his head and left him unable to move. "I was in a moment seized with a fit that deprived me of a sense and motion and left me no other sign of life than that of breathing. I suppose it was of the apoplectic kind. It lasted for about an hour, and when I recovered it left a pain and dizziness in my head that continued."

Unemployed for months, he studied the Bible and began to spend time with progressive leaders of both the Anglican and Independent wings of the English Reformation. As his strength returned, he taught himself Greek and Hebrew. Then, as he immersed himself into the Gospels, he began to wonder if God was calling him to preach.

Eight full months after the attack, Newton's savings were gone. Unable to find work at sea, he finally secured a position as the Liverpool tide surveyor. Yet even while he inspected incoming and outgoing cargo, carefully detailing each shipment for the port, he spent more and more time in Bible study. Now convinced that God had saved him from the hurricane for a real purpose, he persuaded a friend to allow him to present a lay sermon at a church in White Chapel.

Newton spent weeks preparing, carefully organizing and reorganizing his message of salvation and promise. Yet as he stepped up to the pulpit on that Sunday in 1758, the thirty-three-year-old man could not read the words he had written on the paper he set on the pulpit in front of him. His knees shaking, he felt as powerless as he had when the storm hit the *Greyhound*.

"Before I had spoken ten minutes," he later wrote, "I was stopped like Hannibal upon the Alps. My ideas forsook me; darkness and confusion filled up their place. I stood on a precipice and could not advance a step forward. I stared at the people and they at me. Not a word more could I speak but was forced to come down and leave the people, some smiling, some weeping. My pride and self-sufficiency were sorely mortified."

He spent the next two months in thought and prayer. He wrote about his doubts, fears, and desires to preach in a journal he called *Miscellaneous Thoughts*. The theme of this small book was little more than an attempt to examine the contents of his heart. As he wrote, he discovered that his soul was as foreign to him as his faith. It seemed he really knew little about either. His salvation was an experience of logic, not one of passion. Thus in most ways he was very much spiritually lost. Still, forty-two days later he asked the Church of England to accept him as a priest. Because of his failure in his one attempt to preach, he was rejected, although his past activities as a slave trader would have surely caused the church leaders to just as rapidly turn down his request. It would take seven more years, and a change of heart about the nature of slavery, before the door to preaching the Word was finally opened to him.

What dramatically changed Newton was the realization of what salvation meant. It was not being plucked from a raging storm or giving up vices; rather it was about the way God lived in his actions. When Newton realized that change was a matter of heart, not mind, he fully embraced the fact that God had not just saved his life but also saved his soul. This led to a trust in God that allowed him to take steps in faith, which included getting back into the pulpit as a layman and sharing his testimony. With faith in his heart, no longer did he freeze. The words he felt flew easily from his lips.

With the change in his heart now obvious, in April 1764 Newton received deacon's orders, and he finally became a priest on June 17. His course was now firmly set.

From his initial day on the job, the now fully saved former sailor was a wonderful pastor. He cared for his flock as a shepherd tends his sheep. He was gentle, kind, and compassionate, traits he had not exhibited when at sea. In fact, when former crewmen ran into Newton, they scarcely recognized him. Yet scores of these hardened men, who had cursed and spat upon other preachers, now listened to Newton. After he gave his testimony, many even fell to their knees and accepted Christ. Soon his church was filled with men who in the past had scoffed at faith. It took a sinner who was once like them to change their perspectives and reach their hearts.

Newton's success was due in no small part to his ability to freely share his past with others. Rather than hide his flaws, transgressions, and sins, he wore them out in the open, showing others just how deeply he had fallen into depravity before God saved him. He argued that if God could bring grace to the old slave trader, a man who had watched hundreds die in the bowels of his ship and tossed their lifeless bodies into the sea, then that same Lord could save anyone. Though his voice and style did not resonate with dynamic charisma, thousands flocked to his church because they could identify with a preacher who did not hold himself above even the vilest drunkard or most immoral prostitute.

So when Newton sang "Amazing Grace" for the first time on January 1, 1773, many were so deeply moved that tears rushed to their eyes. They had never heard a hymn so personal and filled with such raw emotion. Here, clearly presented in this song, was what they needed. It was grace that God offered each of them as they struggled through the storms of life. That was the message of Newton's New Year's Day address, and it was a message that would not just carry his flock through the fresh year but also carry millions since to the faith Newton himself struggled for so long to accept.

John Newton would live another thirty-four years. During that time he would lead thousands to the Lord with his messages and songs. Three decades after illness forced him to give up trading in human cargo, Newton penned his *Thoughts upon the African Slave Trade*, noting that in the world of commerce nothing was "so iniquitous, so cruel, so oppressive, so destructive, as the African Slave Trade!" In fact, he was the guiding force behind William Wilberforce's leading the abolitionist movement in England. Thanks in no small part to Newton, slavery would be outlawed in the United Kingdom and eventually in the United States.

In 1806 Newton was all but blind and still preaching. As he felt the end coming, he said, "I commit my soul to my gracious God and Saviour, who mercifully spared and preserved me, when I was an apostate, a blasphemer, and an infidel, and delivered me from the state of misery on the coast of Africa into which my obstinate wickedness had plunged me; and who has been pleased to admit me to preach his glorious gospel."

He was looking toward Christmas in 1807 when he told friends, "My memory is nearly gone, but I remember two things, that I am a great sinner, and that Christ is a great Saviour."

Newton's tombstone reads, "John Newton, Clerk, once an infidel and libertine, a servant of slaves in Africa, was, by the rich mercy of our Lord and Saviour Jesus Christ, preserved, restored, pardoned, and appointed to preach the faith he had long labored to destroy."

In truth his life can be clearly divided into two separate books. The first is about a man without faith. The second is about a man who not only gains faith but also uses his past sins to pave the road to faith for others. In his first life John Newton was a liar, but in the second he was honest and direct. His personal testimony, found in the words of what is now known as a simple gospel song, has no doubt saved more souls than any sermon ever written. It is this story, the tale of a man who sank into the depths of hell itself and was pulled up by faith, that inspired "Amazing Grace." In that song Newton fully presents the ultimate price of Jesus' dying on the cross in such simple form that it is universally understood.

3

CHARLES ALBERT TINDLEY
Overcoming the Odds

The Civil War might have been over, but the sense of desperation and gloom created by America's bloodiest conflict still hung in the air like a gigantic ghost, haunting every element of society. Among the thousands who had given their lives in the War between the States was a man who had the courage to release the nation from its most dreadful blight—slavery. And just when the light appeared ready to wash away the darkness, Booth shot Lincoln and fear once again became the watchword of the day. Men in white hoods rode through the country, burning crosses, homes, and even former slaves. The freedom that had come with emancipation had placed many southern African-Americans in greater harm while giving them less security than they had known when they were considered nothing more than property. Resentment ran deep, opportunities were few, and promises of a better life rang hollow. What should have been the best of times had seemingly morphed into the worst of times. There were no dreams, no heroes, and little hope.

Charles Albert Tindley was one of those who knew this fear. The teenager constantly looked over his shoulder as he made his way to work each day. Frightened, uneducated, and unprepared for a world that neither welcomed nor wanted him, he yearned to dream but lived in nightmares. During his waking hours all he thought about was working long enough to make enough money for food and shelter. Survival was his goal, and beyond that little else mattered.

And then he saw it.

He first spotted it while walking back to the shack he shared with his aunt. He was dirty, tired, and thirsty after twelve hours in a cotton field, darkness was coming, and he should have moved on. The last thing he wanted was to be caught alone on the road at night. But it was there, he had seen it, and he could almost hear it calling out to him. Should he pick it up? Surely no one wanted it. After all, it looked as though someone had just crumpled it up and tossed it into the weeds. As if he had been grabbed by the collar, Charles stopped, studied that scrap of paper from a distance, and then after glancing over his shoulder to make sure no one was watching, walked over, picked it up, and straightened it out.

What is it? he wondered. Can it be important? Maybe it is a message from God. What does it say? Does it contain words that will direct the rest of my life?

Carefully sticking that torn page into the waistband of his pants, he vowed to find the answer to his questions. When his aunt couldn't read it, he turned to his neighbors, but they were no help at all. So he spent the next few days searching for someone who could solve the mystery. Yet no matter whom he sought out, the answer was always the same: "Who knows and who cares?" But the teen did care. He wanted to know what was written on the paper; in fact, he had to know. So he never went anywhere without the yellowing page and spent hours studying it, as if just staring at the words could somehow unlock their meaning.

This curious, ebony-colored teen was born in Berlin, Maryland, on July 7, 1851. His father had been a slave, a hard-working man who toiled twelve hours a day and six days a week for little more than room and board. He was sold and resold many times, and the elder Tindley would die with little more than he had at birth, laid to rest in a casual fashion that labeled him a soulless piece of property.

Charles's mother, Hester Miller, was a free black woman. Yet her freedom meant little. Everywhere she traveled, she was required to prove she wasn't a slave, producing papers she could not read while praying each time that someone would not claim her as their slave. So even with the legal proof of freedom, she was still treated as a second-class citizen.

In this hostile, bitterly poor world, Charles took his initial steps and learned his first words. It was a bleak existence. When he was four, Hester died, and things grew even worse for the boy.

Charles was raised by plantation servants, and until the conclusion of the Civil War was thought of as a slave. He was fifteen when he was finally told that African-Americans had been freed. Initially the thought of freedom raised his hopes, but then reality set in. The nation's doors were not going to open up to blacks; neither were schools, stores, hospitals, or hotels. In fact, his newfound freedom took away the only two sure things he had ever known: a roof over his head and food on the table.

Standing more than six feet tall, with broad shoulders and rippling muscles, Charles hired himself out plowing the very same fields he had once tilled as a slave. Fourteen hours a day, six days a week, he worked for barely enough to purchase bacon, flour, and a bed. He was sure that this labor was his past, his present, and his future.

And then that piece of paper changed everything.

Several weeks after Charles found the scrap of paper, a man told him of a night school for former slaves. It was ten miles away, but he would be welcome there. To a teenager with no horse and little free time, a ten-mile trip at night might as well have been a journey of a thousand miles. Yet the need to know trumped the impossibility of it all.

One evening after finishing his chores, his heart full of hope, the barefoot teenager ran through the darkness from his home to that school. What was the message on that paper? He had to find out.

To his dismay, he discovered that the paper was nothing more than a flyer for a local sale. Yet even though this was not the message from God he had longed for, as the words were read to him, he still memorized them. And the next night he ran back again, this time to find out what was written on the pages of a book he had seen a child reading at that same school. And every night that followed, he kept coming back to unravel the mysteries of the English language. Ultimately it was not Lee surrendering to Grant that bought this young man's freedom; it was a meaningless scrap of paper that set Charles Tindley free.

Several months later, on a Sunday morning walk, Charles heard a choir singing inside a tiny frame building. He peeked into a window and saw scores of African-American sharecroppers sitting on homemade benches, singing about God. He yearned to go inside, to hear more, to raise his voice with theirs, yet his ragged clothing and muddy feet held him back. Racing down to a nearby creek, he washed his feet in the water, dried them with grass and leaves, and returned. He carefully opened the church door and was horrified as the squeaky hinges announced his arrival. Everyone in the church turned to see who was coming in so late. Charles wanted to run, but fright and embarrassment held him in place. Turning his eyes from the congregation's stares, the large, awkward, ill-kempt young man sought a seat on the back pew. Yet the scores of eyes did not leave him until the pastor's assertive voice demanded their attention.

Picking up the church's only Bible, the older, gray-headed man lovingly held the tattered book and announced, "Our Scripture today is from Matthew. Is there anyone here who can read from God's Word?"

The people anxiously looked from one to another. Men and women shrugged, shook their heads, and murmured, but no one raised a hand. Like the pastor, they were illiterate. Finally, after the preacher had studied all the others, his eyes fell on Charles.

"Can you read?" he quietly asked.

"Yes," Charles whispered in reply.

"Then will you come to the front and read the Scripture for us?"

Shyly Tindley got up and shuffled to the aisle. As he again felt the congregation's stares, he rued his bare feet and his torn, dirty clothes. At that moment it felt as if God himself had called him into this place to embarrass him. Why had he walked in? Why had he put himself in this position?

Yet he continued to move forward. When he finally stood in front of the pulpit, the preacher stepped aside and pointed to the open Bible. In a quivering voice Charles began.

"For I was hungry ..."

Immediately hands shot into the air and amens were shouted. Looking up, Charles realized that he was the reason for this sudden joy. The church had been looking for a person who could read this book. He was an answer to their prayers. In this clapboard building filled with the very poorest of the poor, Charles, through faith and accepting Christ as his savior, found the freedom of salvation and in the process heard the first inkling of a calling. Yet just like the long run to the rural school, the trip to realizing God's vision would be neither easy nor short.

Charles continued to attend the church, reading Scripture to a crowd hungry to hear and understand those sacred words. Later the teen led prayers and sang hymns. And at the age of seventeen in that same church he also married Daisy Henry.

As his faith grew, those in the tiny congregation urged Charles to give in to the call to preach. Yet while the passion for the Bible and sharing the wonder of faith with others was alive in his heart, at that time Charles could no more understand God's plan for his life than he could read the scrap of paper when he first found it along the road. What he did understand was that a black man with a wife had little hope of ever escaping poverty in rural Maryland. His first step of faith had been going into the tiny church that became his spiritual home. His second step was leaving that congregation to seek a new life in Philadelphia.

In the decade after the Civil War, Philadelphia was a city where newly freed slaves were welcomed with certain restrictions. They could work in the city, live in an area "reserved" for them, build churches and schools, but they were also expected to not mix in the white man's world. In other words, they had to "understand their place." If they didn't, the legal authorities would step in. Thus while Charles would find a job, the open society promised after the end of the war was still closed to him and all like him.

Charles wanted to preach, but the economic reality of having a growing family forced him to use his massive frame rather than his growing brain to put food on the table. With no real vocational skills, he obtained a job as a hod carrier, mixing and delivering mortar and other supplies to bricklayers. He also found work as the janitor for the John Wesley Methodist Episcopal Church. This second job would be as providential as finding the scrap of paper.

John Wesley Methodist Episcopal Church was the black community's most progressive, dynamic, and evangelical congregation in Philadelphia. It often served as a gathering point for some of the greatest African-American speakers and thinkers of the era. The men and women who shared their faith, life experiences, and dreams in the church prompted Charles to delve deeper into his own thinking and understanding of economics, law, politics, and Scripture. Over the next decade, he devoted all his spare time to reading every book in the church's library as well as studying theological courses from the Boston School of Theology and learning Hebrew from a Jewish rabbi. Yet even with his growing knowledge, he would be middle-aged before he finally surrendered to the call to preach. And the parishes that called him were so small that he still had to maintain employment in the secular world.

In 1902, virtually unknown outside his small parishes, and at fifty-one, several years beyond the average life expectancy of a hard laborer, Charles was called to fill the pulpit at the church where he had been a janitor. Accepting the position as pastor of

John Wesley was a dream come true for the former slave, but the welcome he received when he first stood to address the congregation would be his greatest test of faith since he walked barefoot into a tiny rural church as a teen. Once again every eye was on him, seemingly waiting for him to make a mistake. A few, insulted by having a janitor leading the service, walked out. Over the next few weeks, meetings were called and Tindley was asked to produce his high school and college diplomas. Just as he had once not had the proper clothes to wear to church, now he had no academic records to produce. All he had to give was what he had learned on his own. In the face of the ridicule, it would have been easiest to give up. Yet he had once known real slavery, so he was not going to allow himself to be chained by others' expectations now. He was sure God had called him, and he knew he had something to offer. So he would not resign. Instead he readied his sermons, even as the congregation slipped to a few hundred, and he continued to stand firm in his faith.

Though he loved books and constantly studied the Bible, Charles Tindley, unlike most of his learned peers, found the greatest inspiration for his messages in what he witnessed as he walked down Philadelphia's crowded streets. Here, among abandoned children, prostitutes, gamblers, drunks, and con men of all races, he saw those who needed the message of hope, compassion, and salvation. But how could a former slave and janitor convince his small congregation to embrace this new concept of being a church for all men, no matter their color, their station in life, or their lack of social skills? To him this kind of ministry was a clear, vivid, dynamic, and living vision, but how could he share it with others? He had no means. In that way he was still the boy who could not read the scrap of paper.

Charles used his messages to teach that being pure and faithful wasn't enough. Christians, even those who were being oppressed by the world, should also reach out to others. "You've never seen a peach tree eat its own peaches," he explained, "but you have seen a tree so laden with fruit that its branches reached the ground so a toddler can pick and partake. Our lives should be like that tree. Not what we maintain for ourselves, but [what we] give to others, as God gave his Son. I want to be like that tree, serve others, share what I can with others."

He wanted the church he led to become like that tree. Yet it would take a special holiday sermon for this message to really take root.

During the Christmas season, Charles stopped in front of a church and watched through a window as a man on a ladder untied gifts from a decorated Christmas tree and gave these gifts to families sitting in pews. Overcome by this scene, Tindley could now clearly see what God had written on his page of life. Hurrying back to his study, he scribbled down a message called "Heaven's Christmas Tree." This message would begin a movement and set the foundation of another preacher's dream more than five decades later.

Tindley explained to his flock of a few hundred that God wanted his children to present the following gifts. The first was "hope for the hopeless." The next was "forgiveness for the guilty." Then there was "help to the weak," "friendship for the friendless," and "peace for a troubled soul." And he concluded his message by presenting the need for Christians to provide "homes for the homeless." He acknowledged to his small flock that the challenge of providing the world with these gifts was great, but if they as a church body would commit themselves to living this charge, then they could not only reach more people but also bring a bit of heaven down to earth.

Charles, who had once been embarrassed at being a poor, ignorant former slave, now embraced those elements from his past. The bonds of oppression and poverty he had known might have delayed his mission, but they had not held him back. He had refused to give in to them. He had found a way to read, found a way to learn, and found a way to discover his mission in life. Still, he was acutely aware that the hard life facing most poor people, both black and white, gave them little hope, comfort, or joy. Most felt trapped. They knew they would never have riches or be given equal rights. Not as strong as Tindley, most had grown to accept their lot as second-class citizens, and their spirits had been partly broken. But surely if they saw how he had triumphed over the odds — he, a man who had come from a place even lower than where they had begun — then they would have the faith to follow.

Realizing he had to be the first to act on his message, the preacher left the confines of his small office and made his way into the streets of the city. At a time when most black Americans tried to keep a low profile, an inspired Tindley stood tall and walked into the offices of the city's most successful politicians, business owners, and bankers. He looked the mayor in the eye and demanded funds to help the "least of these" of all ages. When most people in the white community turned him down or laughed him off, he organized banks, trade unions, and employment agencies, using his and his congregation's limited resources to jump-start these enterprises. As these institutions flourished, the mayor and the white business sector took a second look at the black community and got involved. Charles even used some of their gifts to turn his sanctuary into a feeding and housing center for the poor and homeless.

To further live out the lessons of his sermons, the preacher strolled the streets each day seeking out beggars, giving them both food and spiritual guidance. He walked into bars and bordellos, where he witnessed without judging. He found families who would keep homeless children. He organized education programs for illiterate adults. And he didn't stop where the black community ended. He went into every part of Philadelphia with a message so powerful, he was able to transcend race at a time when nothing and no one else could do so.

Now hundreds who had known little but pain, those who really were "the least of these," were coming to hear him preach. These men and women wanted to know when things were going to get better, when they were going to have a chance at getting ahead. They wanted to know when the world was going to be fair. They wanted to know when the black man was going to stand beside the white man on level ground.

Tindley couldn't give his people a timetable. Nowhere in the Scriptures could he find a place that spelled out the answers the former slaves and the children of former slaves wanted to know. And he realized that his sermon's message would be quickly forgotten. But music had a way of living on. So through a song he composed, the preacher found a way to address his people's struggles.

> *Trials dark on every hand, and we cannot understand*
> *All the ways that God would lead us to the blessed promised*
> *   land.*
> *He will guide us with his eyes and we'll follow 'til we die,*
> *And we'll understand it better by and by.*

After Tindley first sang "When the Morning Comes" on a Sunday morning in 1904, he reminded his people that the twelve disciples who followed Christ also wanted immediate answers. They too wanted to level the ground and have power placed in their hands. They too grew tired of the trials. But they had to wait. He then reminded his listeners he had to wait more than fifty years to fully realize his own calling. Keep the faith, he told them, and you will find the answers. And more kept coming back to hear Philadelphia's man of action.

Soon almost half of those who gathered to hear Tindley preach on Sunday were white. Prominent white seminaries of the day even sent their students to listen to his sermons. Realizing he was now being studied and his influence could reach places no black man had ever gone, he vowed to find new ways to present an old story.

Remembering what first drew him into church, he began to pepper his services with classical music and old slave spirituals. Unlike other pastors who just added them for flavor, he used them to create moods and set up his sermons. And after the reception he received from "When the Morning Comes," he also composed more songs, ones that had a new personal feel, like John Newton's "Amazing Grace," rather than the corporate message about God that was found in older hymns.

A combination of powerful sermons, exciting new music, and revolutionary programs that reached into the black and white communities fulfilled his vision as it fueled growth. In four short years Tindley's once small church had become one of the largest in Pennsylvania, and its influence reached deep into city hall. By 1906 the congregation had grown to over five thousand members.

The former slave could now go anywhere in the city and be accepted by most as an equal. Those who still could not abide the color of his skin nevertheless understood his power and influence. Thus when he spoke, they listened. Yet beyond his ministry in the city that now held him in awe, it was his music that took his message to the world. Through songs like "Stand by Me," people of all colors were coming to know the faith that had paved the way for a poor, uneducated black man to speak to thousands of people of all colors several times a week. It was Tindley, more than any other preacher, who first put the individual face-to-face with a God who saw no one's color, only one's soul. It was the big man with a dream who brought the world American gospel music.

Tindley's stature did not diminish as he aged. His church grew to more than ten thousand, and his charity outreach touched hundreds of thousands of all races each year. Heads of state and royalty came to meet with him in his own home and on his own terms. He spoke in hundreds of white churches, essentially breaking the color line time and time again. And when he died in 1933, tens of thousands came to testify that by clinging to faith, not only had

Tindley overcome all the obstacles in his own life, but he had made it possible for them to achieve many of their dreams as well.

Yet this former slave's influence did not end on the day he drew his last breath. The chains he had broken, the walls he had torn down, the respect he had gained through his own stubborn faith and dreams, would impact an even greater movement three decades after his death. After an especially compelling message in 1903, Charles Albert Tindley sang a song he had penned for those who faced prejudice, pain, and suffering in their own lives. On that day, in front of a few hundred, in a deep baritone Tindley sang for the first time "I Shall Overcome." Little did he know that his gospel song, meant to inspire and encourage his small flock, would become the anthem for the civil rights movement some sixty years later.

Tindley was one of the first to dare to throw open the doors and reach out to people of all colors. He broke countless color lines long before Jackie Robinson put on the uniform of the Brooklyn Dodgers. He dreamed dreams not just for himself but for all who had been oppressed, and then he found ways to reach out and inspire the "least of these" as well. He gave birth to a form of music that has arguably become the most powerful expression of faith in the world.

And it all started when God dropped a scrap of paper into a former slave's life.

4

CHARLES WESLEY
Setting Faith to Music

As he stared out over the Atlantic Ocean, one thought rested heavily on his mind. Though he was only twenty-eight years old, Charles Wesley was well aware that he was an abject failure. He had been given a chance to pioneer the work of the Church of England in America, and his efforts had proven disastrous. He had converted no Indians and had alienated most of the English settlers in the Georgia colony. He had completely botched his jobs as a missionary, a pastor, and a secretary to the governor. To top it off, he had managed to complete this trio of disasters in less than six months.

Leaning against the ship's railing, his chin resting firmly against his chest, he was ashamed to be coming home to England with no tales of glory to share with his friends and family. He had been so confident he would change the world for Christ and his country, so why had this happened? Where had he gone so wrong?

Just over a year before, in October 1735, after being ordained an Anglican priest by the bishop of London, Charles was sure his life course had been set. He and his brother John were going to travel to the New World and help James Oglethorpe establish Christianity in Georgia. With the blessings of everyone he knew, except his oldest brother Samuel Jr., Charles excitedly packed his belongings, sure that he and John would take the colonies by storm. However, the storm nearly took *them*.

Fierce storms plagued the voyage to America. The boat was violently pitched by waves through much of the journey, and the men grew deathly ill as waves crashed over the decks. For days it appeared the ship would join thousands of others as a forgotten relic at the bottom of the ocean. Panic was everywhere. In fact, the only ones who seemed at peace were German immigrants who called themselves Moravian Brothers. These followers of Martin Luther appeared to have no worries. Even as they were tossed across the decks, often clinging to ropes to keep from being washed overboard, these travelers never seemed concerned about their fate. During a calm between storms, a curious and shaken Charles approached one of the group's leaders.

"Aren't you frightened?" he asked.

The simply dressed man gently smiled and said, "No, we are not."

"And your women and children," Charles inquired, "aren't they scared?"

The man shook his head. "We have no fear of death. Christ has taken that fear away from us. If the ship sinks, we will join him in heaven. If we arrive in the New World, he will greet us there. He is with us and has been since we let him into our hearts."

The Anglican priest was amazed by the man's calm, secure, and personal faith. The powerful storms had no effect on him. He rode through the waves as if Jesus were standing right beside him. This was a faith Charles could not comprehend, yet it was also one that drew him in like a moth to the flame. This kind of deity was as foreign to Charles as was his American destination. Their God had a personality, a breath, and even a form. Thus for the remainder of the trip, whenever he had the chance, Charles engaged the group in conversation, trying to understand why their God seemed so real and near to them while his God was so vague and distant.

On March 9, 1736, John and Charles Wesley arrived in Savannah fully expecting to stay in Georgia for the remainder of their lives. Yet the spring heat and humidity, in addition to the coarse and "un-English" behavior of the colonists, caused both men to question why God had led them to this strange world.

In the minds of the Wesleys, there was simply no order or discipline in America. No one was interested in following the proper, established, and time-honored English customs or even the rules of the Anglican Church. These people drank, smoked, and even worked on Sunday. They allowed laypeople to conduct worship services and baptize converts.

Charles, whose religious philosophy was as rigid as his proper use of the King's English, felt he had to bring structure to at least the way these pioneers treated matters of faith. So when given control of the church at St. Simon's Island, he set to work enforcing the laws and edicts of the Church of England. He deemed it was time for these people to act like Christians. If they didn't, he was sure their next voyage would take them straight to hell.

From the beginning things did not go well. One of Charles's first acts was tossing a doctor in jail for hunting on the Sabbath. This action caused a woman to lose a baby because the physician was not free to help in the difficult childbirth. Yet even the death of a child did not affect Charles's zeal for making sure every rigid law of the church was strictly embraced. His fervent actions destroyed any chance he had at building a bridge to the local community. In a matter of a few weeks he was reviled by almost everyone on the island.

Relieved of his church duties, Charles was given new assignments, but he fared no better as a secretary to Oglethorpe or as a missionary to the Indians. Soon few in the colony would speak to him, and some even started rumors about his personal conduct in an attempt to have him sent back to the Old World. Within two months things had grown so bad that the man who provided lodging for Charles gave away his bed, and no one in Savannah would build him a new one.

In May Charles was informed it would be best if he gave up his missionary work with the Indians and resigned his position as the governor's secretary. Now unemployed, he was forced to depend upon his older brother's goodwill just to eat. On July 26, when Oglethorpe needed someone to return to England and give a report on the progress of the colony, a desperate Charles volunteered for the duty. Yet even that seeming stroke of good fortune turned into an ordeal.

The ship he booked passage on was ancient and manned by an inexperienced crew. He was stuck in both Charlestown and Boston for weeks as repairs were made on the vessel in an attempt to make it seaworthy. It was still leaking badly when it finally left New England in the fall. The delay meant the tiny vessel would be fighting winter storms for weeks while trying to cross the North Atlantic. After avoiding disaster more times than Charles could count, the ship arrived at Deal on the third day of December.

Back home, a relieved Charles was a safe but still very lost soul. Walking on firm English soil and seeing old friends only proved to reinforce that point. A year before, he felt his life's work would be installing the Anglican standard on the American population. Now his credibility was shattered and his future as a clergyman seemed bleak. He assumed he would spend the remainder of his days as a teacher for those wealthy enough to go to one of England's schools of higher education. It was not something he wanted to do, but it seemed to be his only option.

In August of 1737 Charles finished his final duties for Oglethorpe by convincing the governor's financial supporters that the colony in Georgia was doing well. Again unemployed, he consulted with several noted church leaders about the direction he should take in life. In almost all of these conversations, Charles told the story of the Moravians who had shown such great courage when riding out storms at sea. Like him, few in the Anglican Church of the time understood the way these "reformers" worshiped or saw God. Many of these scholars argued that the Germans, like the local Baptists, were lost. What they needed was not faith but order. They needed to understand that the way to heaven was paved by keeping church laws, adhering to the ancient practices, studying the great theological essays, and doing good works. Only in this manner could true grace be found. On the surface Charles agreed, but for reasons he didn't comprehend, he still envied the Moravians.

The son and grandson of Anglican priests, Charles turned to prayer in seeking answers. Yet the written prayers he recited and the impersonal pleas he made to the Lord rang hollow. In fact, his intellectual method of searching for peace was now failing to interest him as much as it had failed to interest those he had once tried to lead in Georgia. Even by using the wisdom of the great men he knew, he still could not find any spiritual footing. During this time of upheaval and uncertainty, he met another Moravian who would engage not just his curiosity but also his heart.

Peter Böhler was a German who, for business reasons, needed to become more fluent in English. He employed Charles as his tutor. As the two became friends, they began to discuss the differences in their faith. Böhler suggested various texts to shed some light on the personal way he viewed his relationship to Christ. Reading Martin Luther's view of Galatians, and other theologians' concepts of grace, did not make an immediate impression on the intellectual priest, but it did open a door. Yet it would take a serious illness to finally bring Charles to his knees.

Making little income through tutoring, Charles could not afford lavish surroundings. He found lodging in the humble home of a local mechanic named John Bray. When Charles grew violently ill, Bray often stayed by his bedside, feeding him soup, telling stories, and reciting Scripture. Bray, like Böhler and the Moravians Charles had encountered on the trip to America, was an enthusiastic Christian. He saw his Savior as being very much alive, and he even claimed he felt God's presence when he prayed. He also eagerly spoke of how much the Lord had done in his life. And even though he had been too busy making a living at his craft to become a missionary, keep the ritual times of prayer, or study all the specific edicts and laws of the Anglican Church, the mechanic was sure he was one of God's children and had a home reserved in heaven. This foreign way of thinking opened up debates between the two men, but no argument Charles presented on church rituals could dent Bray's steadfast resolve that he had been saved and that his salvation could never be lost.

On Pentecost Sunday, May 21, 1738, as Bray spoke of a risen Christ who had died for people's sins, Charles Wesley felt something move not in his mind but in his heart. With no warning, all around him he sensed God as he never had before. He knew this presence had to be the Holy Spirit; he just could not fully believe that it could still be an empowering force in the modern world. Yet when it didn't pass, he knew something was going on. Suddenly feeling strength rush through his sick and weakened body, he leaped out of bed. Grabbing his host, he earnestly proclaimed, "I believe, I believe."

As if shocked by his emotional declaration, Charles paused for a moment, catching his breath before dramatically announcing, "My sins are finally covered."

Though he had been too feeble to even rise from bed a few minutes before, he now stood upright and boldly announced, "My faith has let me stand, my faith is keeping me from falling. Yes, I am weak, but I am confident of Christ's protection."

Just like the men and women he had met on his journey to America, Wesley was now sure it was faith that secured his salvation. Thus failing in his American adventure was not going to keep him out of heaven. Even if he never achieved any kind of success, he was still saved!

For the next two days Charles was so excited that he could barely eat or sleep, but miraculously, in spite of his spartan diet, his strength fully returned. Rising from the bed that had been his home for weeks, he sat at a writing table. Even though he had never before attempted to compose a song, he felt moved to write about his conversion experience. First he quickly scratched down a thought that was filling his heart: "He [God] put a new song in my mouth." Then he dashed out his testimony in verse form.

> And can it be that I should gain
> an interest in the Savior's blood!
> Died he for me? who caused his pain!
> For me? who him to death pursued?
> Amazing love! How can it be
> that thou, my God, shouldst die for me?
> Amazing love! How can it be
> that thou, my God, shouldst die for me.

He almost didn't share his salvation song. He strongly considered tucking it in his Bible and keeping it to himself. The message was that personal. But as a tribute to the man who had led him to what he would call his "second birth," Charles sang it to Bray. Overwhelmed by the power of the lyrics, Bray encouraged him to share it with others.

Charles's first chance to sing the hymn to someone other than Bray was on May 24, when he was surprised by a visit from his brother John. Like Charles, the older Wesley had washed out as a missionary in the New World. A disillusioned John had also come back with more questions than answers. He too had become unsure of the direction he now needed to take in his life and work.

Then, just three days after Charles had truly been saved, John also discovered the power of being justified by faith. At ten o'clock in the evening, he raced into Bray's house, found Charles, and declared, "I believe." Suddenly both brothers had a new calling. As they spoke, Charles realized that everything that had happened to them up to this point had been necessary for their conversion. The old life had been the foundation of this new one. God had charted this course since he took his first breath.

Charles almost hadn't survived his birth. Born two months premature, he was so tiny that few felt he would live more than a couple hours. In fact, for more than eight weeks he did not make a sound or open his eyes. The eighteenth child of Samuel and Susannah Wesley, he survived his first year only by his mother's prayers and her constant attention. Those prayers would continue throughout his youth, as Susannah became his spiritual tutor. The devoted Anglican pastor's wife felt it was her duty to teach her children Bible stories as a way of providing them with the moral backbone to be upstanding members of British society. It was she who also taught them the proper Anglican prayers.

Charles's father, who led the Epworth community church, fancied himself a poet and tried to pass his love of verse on to his children. He also acted as their instructor in history, math, and writing. Like his wife, he attempted to shelter his children from the ills of a world seemingly gone mad by encouraging them to seek refuge in the church.

England in the early 1700s was chaotic. Even though judges imposed very harsh sentences for even minor offenses, crime was rampant. There were so many public hangings that these executions had fostered a thriving business in souvenirs, concessions, and sideshows. Every sixth building in London was a pub. The consumption of alcohol was such an accepted practice that gin was given to babies to keep them quiet so their mothers could party. Prostitutes were as common on the streets as newspaper vendors, and thousands of children were abandoned each year, becoming members of dangerous rogue gangs who preyed upon anyone they met. It was simply a horrible period to raise a family. Yet this was the world Charles saw every day of his youth.

What probably saved Charles was his oldest brother, Samuel Jr., becoming a teacher at the Westminster School. This rare opportunity for formal education paved the way for Charles, in 1716, to follow in the footsteps of his brother John and enter the sheltered world usually reserved only for the children of the very wealthy. He proved to be such a good student that five years later he won the King's Scholar award and then, in 1721, was accepted to Christ Church, Oxford University, where he became one of the few children from a lower-class home to have the chance to gain a college degree.

During his initial year of study, Charles was anything but a model citizen. Oxford's students had long had a sordid reputation. Organized into various social clubs, the students threw huge parties, where group members drank, gambled, and even hired prostitutes as "hostesses." The twenty-year-old Charles plunged into this lifestyle, relishing his freedom. When word got back to his parents of his behavior, they sent John to straighten him out. When his older brother informed Charles of his duty to live up to the family's Christian code, the younger Wesley answered, "What, would you have me to be a saint all at once?" He would not stop his partying ways until his second year at Oxford, when he began to study the theological elements of Anglican faith.

When confronted by the serious nature of a Christian lifestyle, Charles gave up his riotous behavior to embrace the more sobering task of fully understanding the edicts of the Church of England. This change was so dramatic that few of his friends could now recognize him. His studies created a belief that the official church of the state was solid in its principles but weak in its conduct. The more he learned about the meaning of Christ's commandments, the more Charles felt the church had largely become a social outlet for mumbling Christian thoughts. Church leaders were ignoring the tenets of faith they were expected to follow. He was sure things needed to change in order to put the church back on solid footing and give parishioners the tools needed to get to heaven.

Charles began to keep all the various church rules to the letter and attend the weekly sacrament. He prayed at the times it was ordained he pray. He read the words the rules said he should read, at the moment they said he should read them. During a period when most Anglican priests were failing to go through the motions required of them as church leaders, Charles was doing it all. He was so rigid in his worship practices and studies that he gained the nickname The Methodist, meaning the one who was methodical in his study of the Bible and in his worship of the Lord. He continued this type of practice, drawing many others to his strict philosophy, including his brother John, until he graduated with an MA in 1732.

Both of the Wesley brothers had become so serious in their efforts to begin a movement to restore the English church to what they felt were the best practices for worship and growth that Charles and John now mirrored each other even in the way they spoke and walked. One of their friends said, "To describe one is to describe them both." Therefore it was hardly surprising that in 1735 they both turned down their father's deathbed request to take over his parish, electing instead to go to the New World to create a foundation of strict adherence to Anglican practices. The brothers assumed it would be much easier to establish the proper practices in the brand-new churches of America than to attempt to change the course of ancient congregations in London. Yet when they were met with rebellion in the colonies, they both came to question their values, self-worth, and calling. The Wesleys were only rescued by the one element they had missed in their study of theology—grace.

After the near-death experience at Bray's home, and now armed with faith won by grace, Charles again took to the pulpit. For two years he spoke in a large number of Anglican churches. This time his message was one of salvation by grace. He dwelled no longer on rituals and laws but on faith. His dismissal of works being the key factor in becoming God's child resonated with the poorer members of congregations but not with the wealthy or the church establishment. The vicar of Islington echoed many of the strongest voices in the Anglican Church when he proclaimed, "Charles should preach in his church no more."

With no churches willing to open their doors to Charles's messages of grace, his ministry appeared to be over. But then George Whitefield, an Anglican priest who like Charles had been expelled from traditional church pulpits, approached him.

Before Wesley's conversion, Whitefield's writings had shocked him. He couldn't understand why Whitefield made controversial comments like, "I am persuaded that the generality of preachers talk of an unknown and an unfelt Christ. The reason why congregations have been so dead is because they have had dead men preaching to them. How can dead men beget living children?"

Now as he stood on the outside of the church looking in, Wesley understood that message. Thus when Whitefield asked him to speak before gatherings in farmers' fields, in city parks, and on street corners, Charles saw it as an opportunity to work in a world that had no limits placed on it by social standing or church dogma.

Overnight the once staid and serious Charles became an emotional evangelist. He was such a dynamic speaker that his messages were often reprinted and distributed as tracts. He was constantly preaching salvation by grace, even going into the prisons to give his message of eternal hope. He became one of the few clergymen willing to take the final steps with condemned men, begging them until the last moment to give their hearts over to the Lord. As they came to understand forgiveness, scores were saved before the hangman's noose was slipped around their neck. Yet as successful as Charles was in jails, his message of faith through grace really took hold in the fields, where he preached to the illiterate, common person.

In his first few outdoor events, Charles spoke to several hundred curious onlookers. These people, most from very poor families, initially looked upon the services as entertainment. Yet as they heard this new kind of gospel preached, as they listened to the songs Charles was writing and singing with his sermons, many were caught up in an understanding that there was a God who actually cared for them and that Jesus had really died for their sins. Scores came forward to embrace this new kind of religion.

Within weeks the crowds had grown to a thousand, and after a few months more than ten thousand showed up anytime they heard that Charles was going to preach. True, he was kicked out of the great cathedrals, but they had limited seating, strict rules of conduct, and only the upper-crust elements of English society. His expulsion became not a sign of failure but a blessing. Outside the church, the preacher could reach those who truly were "the least of these."

Charles was now so lost in his calling that the once distinguished gentleman had evolved into an eccentric. He wore winter clothing year round, rode horses rather than in carriages, moved about the stage like an actor, and fired off questions to his associates with no warning. Speaking four or five times a day, often traveling fifty miles in twenty-four hours, he practiced his sermons while he rode. Thus he often appeared to be babbling to himself.

When he got an idea for a song, he galloped to the nearest home, knocked on the door, and demanded, "Pen and ink! I must have pen and ink!" Once he had written the lyrics that had so gripped his mind, he stuffed the paper into his pocket, excused himself, and got back on his horse to continue on his way. Boldly riding through lightning storms, snow, and gale-force winds, he had become just like the Moravian brothers he had met on his only voyage to America. Yet this strange behavior, while frightening many established church leaders, endeared him to commoners. They sensed that Charles acted as he did because God was so alive in him.

Charles's success began to concern the British establishment. They were worried he might upset the balance of English society. After all, he seemed to be empowering thousands of the poor and illiterate with a message that in God's eyes they were equal even to King George. A few thought this might lead to a rebellion.

Thus organized riots often broke out during Charles's outdoor services. He was pelted with vegetables and rocks and on occasion was knocked off platforms by fists. Yet he continued to preach and sing.

One of his songs that probably led to more conversions than all of his inspired sermons was "O, For a Thousand Tongues to Sing." It was based on something he had once heard John Bray say: "If I had a thousand tongues I would use all of them to sing praises to my Lord." Hundreds of other inspired songs quickly followed.

Almost forty, Charles was the Billy Graham of his day when he married Sarah Gwynne. Though Sarah's face had been disfigured by a childhood bout with smallpox, Charles felt she was the most beautiful woman he had ever seen. For the rest of his life, Sarah would stand by him and with her smile and sweet spirit always reflect the faith she embraced as deeply as her husband did. Sarah became more than his wife and the mother of his children; she was the missing element that he needed to fully realize God's perfect love. In his mate, Charles saw Jesus, and if he ever again doubted grace, he only had to look in her eyes.

The message of faith, one that much of the established church had ignored for years, was something people needed and wanted to hear. Thus even though his own church had closed its doors to Charles, beginning in the 1740s a host of other denominations welcomed this new kind of preacher into their sanctuaries. He was amazed as he reported to his family, "The Presbyterians say I am a Presbyterian; the churchgoers that I am a minister of theirs; and the Catholics are sure I am a good Catholic in my heart." The acceptance that had been denied him in America was now with him everywhere because he was trying not to establish rules but to present faith through grace.

About this same time Charles began to publish his songs. The demand for the hymnbooks was so great that the Wesleys found themselves with far more orders than they could deliver. Songs such as "And Can It Be That I Should Gain," "Christ the Lord Is Risen Today," "Come, Thou Long Expected Jesus," "Hark, the Herald Angels Sing," "Jesus, Lover of My Soul," and "Love Divine All Love Excelling" were reaching thousands, not just in England but across Europe and in the place where he had had such a disastrous ministry—America. Within a decade of his "second birth," Charles's musical testimony had become an even more powerful force than his preaching. Millions who would never even see the man would still know his heart, feel his faith, and come to know his Savior through his inspired verse.

By making his music uniquely personal, Charles was also leading a revolution begun by Isaac Watts. These men's songs were the foundation of a much more personal and spiritual church music. For the first time, Christian music was really being written for common people. These hymns took church music out of the control of theologians and gave it directly to those seeking the Lord. Many established church musicians waved these hymns off as "folk songs," and because it was just common folks who initially latched on to them, this view was correct. Charles's songs were not written for the high church he once served; they were written to be sung by those who felt their message of saving grace in their hearts. Because many people could not read, hymns provided these illiterate people with a foundation for understanding. They were tracts that needed no explanation and were easy to share.

As he grew older, Charles could no longer maintain a heavy road schedule, so he founded a small church near his home. A few months later he and John opened a much larger house of worship in a deserted ironworks building in London. The Foundry Meeting House, as they called it, would become the bricks-and-mortar birthplace of the Methodist denomination. It is ironic that a name once used to poke fun at Charles was now attached to the most important evangelical movement of its time.

Charles preached for the remainder of his life. Still, as busy as he was, he found the time to meet with abolitionist William Wilberforce and lend support to his work. He also continued to compose. The day before he took his final breath, he finished the last of his more than 6,500 hymns.

Charles died on March 19, 1788, and though he was considered to be one of the founders of the Methodist movement, he still thought of himself as an Anglican priest. Just before his death he told the rector in nearby St. Marylebone Parish Church, "Sir, whatever the world may say of me, I have lived, and I die, a member of the Church of England. I pray you to bury me in your churchyard." Since by now many of Charles's songs were being used by Anglican congregations, this final wish was quickly granted, and eight Anglican priests were assigned to serve as his pallbearers.

One clergyman noted, "Wesley has not just founded a new denomination, he has woken us up to the need to preach of salvation through faith in all houses of worship." Many of his Anglican brothers were the ones who enthusiastically accepted that wake-up call.

Once an abject failure who had no direction, Charles had been a moral man who embraced religion but had no faith. However, after declaring, "I believe," he would become one of the most important Christian leaders of his era. By his life's end he had emerged as a hero for three unique gifts he gave the world.

The first was his evangelism. Wesley took the Word to the people rather than hoping the people would find their way to the Word. Through the use of outdoor meetings, Charles set in motion a path that would be followed by Dwight L. Moody, Billy Sunday, Billy Graham, and hundreds of others. In a sense, he helped build the foundation of the revival movement.

The second element that has endeared him to millions was his part in founding the Methodist Church. Millions around the globe have met Christ within the walls of one of the congregations that sprang from Charles and John Wesley's movement of faith.

Yet the greatest impact of Charles Wesley has to be his hymns. He was one of the first to move Christian music to the realm of personal testimony. That is probably the reason why more than five hundred of the songs he composed are still being sung today. One theologian wrote, "If we were to lose every Bible in the world, we could pretty accurately rewrite God's Word by going through Charles Wesley's hymns." Even now, more than two hundred and twenty years after his death, the preaching songwriter continues to lead thousands to the Lord through his music. Charles Wesley indeed has been blessed with having a thousand tongues to praise his Lord and Savior. That is a legacy few can match.

5

WESLEY BRANCH RICKEY
Opening the Door

At about the time that Charles Albert Tindley was taking the pulpit for the first time at a church named for Charles and John Wesley, a young man whose first name was Wesley was trying to make his mark in the glamour sport of that era—Major League Baseball.

Wesley Branch Rickey was a rarity in the sporting world of the early twentieth century. He stood out not because of his talents and skills but because he was college educated, didn't drink, and would not play on Sundays. This devout Methodist seemed too cultured and refined to become a central figure in America's great pastime. Yet even though he seemingly had two strikes against him, the twenty-six-year-old Branch desperately wanted to make his mark on the nation's green-turfed diamonds. More than his principle focus, baseball was almost an obsession.

Rickey had first caught scouts' eyes as a catcher at Ohio Wesleyan. In 1903, with his degree in hand, he put off law school and signed with a Class B team in Terre Haute, Indiana. The future Baseball Hall of Famer failed this first test, but rather than give up, he caught a train to Le Mars, Iowa. He played well enough in the corn belt that within two years the St. Louis Browns gave him a shot at the big time. The highlight of his short stint with the team was when he hit two home runs in one game. Other than that, nothing Rickey did proved spectacular.

In 1907 Branch was sold to the New York Highlanders, where the newly signed catcher set a record that has never been broken: allowing thirteen men to steal bases on him in just nine innings. A year later he was out of the big leagues and on his way to Michigan for law school. Few expected to ever see the young man back at any major-league park in any capacity other than as a fan. No one would have predicted that he would eventually revolutionize the game he so deeply loved by changing the outdated and immoral views of a nation.

Wesley Branch Rickey was born five days before Christmas in 1881. He was named for the founding fathers of the Methodist movement, and his middle name also reflected his parents' strong faith. The name Branch was taken from John 15:2: "Every branch in me that beareth not fruit he taketh away: and every branch that beareth fruit, he purgeth it, that it may bring forth more fruit." With that kind of thinking going into the names they chose for their son, it is hardly surprising that Jacob and Emily Rickey taught him more than a thousand Scripture verses before he learned to read.

During Branch's childhood, his world revolved around church, work, and education. Each was stressed as being necessary to make a person whole. Early on he latched on to the motto "Faith without works is dead." This motto guided the remainder of his incredible life. It saw him through more than four decades of failure and brought him courage when he mounted a war with the mindset of an entire nation.

In his hometown Rickey became known as the boy who would do anything for anyone. He was constantly giving of his talents and time to his church, school, and community. Except for one thing, he was the model for all the area youth. If there was one element of his life that many in his congregation and his community took issue with, it was his love of baseball.

Many considered baseball the bastion of drunkards, gamblers, and cheaters. Sermons were delivered warning families that "nothing good could come out of this unholy exercise." Yet the young Rickey wholeheartedly believed that just as a man could be called to preach, he could also be called to play baseball. He felt that his Bible study proved that God wanted good people of character in the world and that they had to be there to change the wrongs of the world. In the game of baseball, he sensed he could make an impact not just with his bat but also with his faith. With the support of his parents, he embraced the game with as much vigor as he did Bible study. Still, many warned that baseball would be his downfall. As he failed with St. Louis and New York, it appeared his critics were right.

When Branch struck out on the playing field, most hoped he would finally give his considerable talents to a much more worthy calling. Yet even while gaining his law degree in Ann Arbor, Rickey took time out to coach the school's baseball team. Though he was a topflight student, the books seemed to always take a back seat to the ball and bat.

By 1913, this time using his law degree, he was back in the big leagues, working in the business office for the St. Louis Browns. His knack for picking out and signing new talent landed him a job as the team's manager. After two subpar seasons, the team suggested that Rickey go back to practicing law. It seemed that he had struck out in baseball for the second time.

During his time away from the game, Branch joined the service and went to war. When he returned to the States from France, he took a train back to St. Louis and convinced the city's other major-league team, the Cardinals, to give him a third chance to make his mark in the big leagues.

For six years Branch managed the team, establishing a pattern that he would use for the remainder of his days in baseball. He quietly encouraged his team members to live clean lives, to read their Bible, and to be role models for young people. The press often took him to task for his convictions, his players usually ignored his prodding, especially when it came to sobriety, and the Cardinals were nothing more than a mediocre group that inspired few in St.

Louis and struck little fear in the hearts of those who played the team. It was no shock when Rickey was finally let go in 1926. Few had tried harder and failed more.

Branch was now forty-five, and the calling he had embraced for more than three decades had done little but bring him pain and disappointment. He was the Job of baseball, a man who meant well but just couldn't garner much more than misery. His lack of success seemed to prove what many in the clergy preached: "God will bless no man who devotes his career to a sinful game."

Rickey's failure appeared complete when his successor as the Cardinals' new manager won the pennant and the World Series in his first season at the helm. If there had ever been a sign, surely this was it. It seemed well past time for Branch to take his wife and family and walk away from the ballpark for the last time.

Yet rather than give up, Branch chose to stay and convinced the Cardinals to move him into the business side of operations. Developing the first team-owned and team-directed minor-league system, he nurtured young players like Pepper Martin and Dizzy Dean. His young project players eventually became the core of the famed Gashouse Gang. Though he would not be their manager, this group he built grew into one of the most dominant teams in baseball. Finally it seemed the curse was over, and his faith in his calling and abilities now appeared justified.

Success in the front office led to Branch's running with a new circle of friends. Movie stars, politicians, clergymen, and the newsmakers of the day were often found sitting beside Rickey at Cardinals games. Many were shocked by the way the man spoke during games. His speech was clean, honest, and direct. His conversations often connected biblical stories with baseball. He quoted Scripture, spoke of faith, and rued the sordid elements of the game he so loved. He still felt that character was more important than batting average. One of his most common themes was what happened to men when they were not at the park playing baseball. He worried over it to such a degree that hundreds heard him say, "How to use your leisure time is the biggest problem of a ballplayer." So those who feared that the game might change Branch had been wrong. In the midst of what so many felt was a sinful world, he was looking for ways to reach the sinners.

One of those who often visited with Rickey was the famed atheistic lawyer Clarence Darrow. They seemed a strange pair: a man who based everything he did in life on having received a call from God, and another who claimed God did not exist. Yet while not understanding the attorney's atheism, Branch had great respect for Darrow. This respect dated back to 1925, when the lawyer made the unpopular decision to represent Ossian Sweet, a black man who had used his gun to defend his home against a band of white bigots. Ironically, the atheist's example would deeply affect the way Rickey viewed baseball, as well as how he would use his Christian convictions to help change it. While it had taken Branch more than three decades to gain success in the game he loved, it would take another ten years for God to reveal his true purpose in calling him to baseball.

In February 1938 Rickey was asked to travel to Chicago to be one of the featured speakers at the two hundredth anniversary of John Wesley's conversion. There Rickey attended a meeting where blacks and whites mingled in the same rooms and ate at the same table. With both races brought together by faith, color suddenly seemed meaningless.

A twenty-five-year-old black preacher who had devoted his life to reaching the slum children of Pasadena, California, made a deep impression on Branch. Karl Everette Downs was the kind of man Rickey wanted to work with and support. While some at the conference were calling Downs a credit to his race, the baseball executive saw him as a credit to the Christian faith and a role model for people of all colors. Meeting and visiting with some of the movers and shakers in the African-American community, especially

Downs, convinced Rickey that American society was ignoring some of its greatest potential by continuing to practice segregation. It was past time for a great change.

Branch's job at the conference was to speak to hundreds of young people. Those who had watched him develop the talent that made the Cardinals champions felt sure that the brash and outspoken Christian leader would find words to uplift and motivate the church's new generation of leaders. He didn't shrink from the challenge. He spoke of witnessing the lure of temptation as he issued his challenge: "We must develop spiritual techniques for tapping sources of power. These include Bible reading as a laboratory manual, small groups sharing fellowship, exploration and mutual support, regular practice of personal devotion, and a constant study of changing social conditions and needs." In other words, Rickey urged them to find a way to reach young people or lose an entire generation.

Rickey's charge was well circulated through the Methodist convention, but few pastors recognized the need for any real change. Most argued that what had worked for generations would continue to work for years to come. This adherence to outdated programs and policies, in both the church and society, surely would have frustrated the revolutionary-minded John and Charles Wesley, and it deeply irritated Rickey. He kept preaching, but few were listening. Things in church and society seemed to be set in stone.

When the United States entered World War II, Branch saw an opportunity to institute dramatic change in baseball. Many of the top stars of the major leagues were entering the military. By the 1942 season, the game was suffering. Rickey pointed out that there was a vast reservoir of talent in the separate Negro leagues, as well as in the Mexican leagues, and these men could bring more excitement and fans to baseball parks. But the ownership in St. Louis laughed. "We have our players, they have theirs. That is the way it should be."

As he sat in the park and glanced into the stands, beyond the fences Rickey noted scores of African-American fans who came out day after day to watch white men play baseball. Many of these men and women had sons who were in the military defending a nation that would not even allow them to be a full part of society. Branch's Christian convictions could no longer quietly allow this to happen. Speaking of what he saw in Sportsman Park, he would later say, "No Negro was permitted to buy his way into the grandstand during that entire period of my residence in St. Louis. The only place a Negro could witness a ball game in St. Louis was to buy his way into the bleachers — the pavilion. With an experience of that kind in back of me, and having had sort of a 'bringing up' that was a bit contrary to that regime, I went to Brooklyn."

The general manager of the Brooklyn Dodgers, Larry MacPhail, had been drafted into military service. Before leaving, he called the now sixty-year-old Rickey and asked him to run the team. This move to New York would be the final element needed for Branch to fully understand why he was called to go into baseball and why his faith had never wavered.

Almost daily Branch drove through neighborhoods divided along racial lines. In a day in which Americans of all ethnic backgrounds were dying in the nation's fight against the Axis powers, Rickey was embarrassed by the prejudice he encountered. It was time for walls to come down and for Americans of all colors to have an equal part in society. He reasoned that if it didn't happen, then we were not a moral nation and we were little better than the nations we were fighting. He argued that the best place to begin this transformation was baseball, and he felt he had the power to do it. It was time for what he would call the Great Experiment.

It was his faith that forced Branch to discount color. If he believed that Jesus died for the sins of all people, then that meant that each person, no matter their race, was equal in the eyes of

God. If that was the case, then as a Christian, Branch had to fully embrace all people and open the eyes of others to that fact as well.

Quietly Rickey began to look at the talent level in the Negro leagues. He sent out scores of scouts to evaluate players. He demanded reports that included not just baseball skills but also a full assessment of moral character. He knew that for his experiment to work, he had to find a man who was not just a great player but also a gentleman with great values. In 1945 he found his man.

Jackie Robinson had been a three-sport star at UCLA and had developed a strong moral code in the church led by Pastor Karl Everette Downs. Branch's respect for Downs might well have been the deciding factor in choosing the all but unknown Robinson over much more proven black ballplayers for his grand experiment. On October 23, 1945, the Dodgers quietly announced that Robinson would join their minor-league team in Montreal.

Before sending Jackie off to Canada, Rickey explained to the young man that his character on and off the field mattered just as much as his prowess at baseball. Robinson left the meeting knowing that his boss wanted him to showcase his Christian values. Jackie didn't let anyone down as he ran away with the International League's Rookie of the Year award and was seen as a fine person of great character.

Branch was a praying man. Those who knew him best were fully aware that he made the major decisions of his life only after seeking a call from God. In the winter of 1947 Rickey prayed a great deal. He also fielded scores of threatening phone calls and received hundreds of angry letters. Politicians, other baseball owners, various members of the clergy, newspaper reporters, and even fans confronted him, demanding that he not try to break the color line. Several Brooklyn players told the GM they would retire rather than play with an African-American. Yet in the face of this firestorm, Rickey did not step back. More than ever he was convinced this action was the reason why God had placed him in baseball, the reason why he had been given so many tests early in his career, and the reason why he had persevered through failure.

On April 12, 1947, the Dodgers purchased Jackie Robinson's contract from the minor leagues. Five days later he became the first African-American to play in the major leagues. Over the next six months, Robinson was verbally abused by players, managers, and fans. No person in the history of the game had ever been treated with as much hostility. Pitchers threw at his head and base runners tried to spike him, but Branch remained in the stands, assuring Robinson that together they could endure whatever happened.

Blessedly, the Great Experiment worked! Robinson was chosen Rookie of the Year, and the Bums, as the Dodgers were called by their fans, even played the mighty Yankees in the World Series. Though hated by millions for doing what he did, Branch was satisfied that he had lived out what his faith demanded of him.

In 1950, with the floodgates open and scores of clubs now accepting African-Americans on their teams, Rickey left Brooklyn to take over the worst team in baseball: the Pittsburgh Pirates. Almost seventy, he had made his mark, opened up the game, and set in motion the integration of an entire society. He could have rested on his laurels and still been lionized as a sports icon and a national hero. Yet the faith that had played such an important part in his life, in every decision he had made, drove him on. He still believed there was something else he needed to do. And because he refused to retire, he was finally able to confront a problem that had tormented him for years.

A letter from a football coach set in motion a movement that would probably impact more young people than anything since the founding of Sunday school. And if Branch Rickey had not still been in baseball, odds are that the movement would have never gotten off the ground.

Don McClannen was a young, energetic World War II veteran who was looking for purpose in his life. While going to college on the G.I. Bill, Don attended a conference in Oklahoma City where a former football coach declared, "A coach can lead kids up a mountain or down the drain, depending on how he lives his life." Don felt a call to be a football coach. Upon graduation the energetic young man took a job at Eastern Oklahoma State College.

The death of a child led Don to look into his own heart. After weeks of prayer, he found his way into an open church and felt touched by God. As a coach, Don had sought out the advice of scores of proven coaches. Now, as a Christian, he began looking for men involved in sports who also embraced faith. Reading all he could find about athletes willing to talk about their Christian convictions created a burning desire to know more. He had to understand how they kept themselves on a high moral plane in the face of the temptations they encountered each day on the road. To find answers, the young coach wrote to each person whose testimony he encountered. Even when he explained that he would drive a thousand miles just to hear their wisdom, no one agreed to a meeting. Yet he continued to write, praying over each letter and hoping that this would be the one that would help him find direction in his own life and secure the meeting with a man who could help him help others in the world of sports.

In 1954 Branch Rickey opened one of Don's letters. Busy trying to rebuild the Pirates, the GM hardly had time to do his job, much less speak to fans. Yet McClannen's sincere words moved him. If this young man wanted to talk about how to merge faith and sports and was willing to drive all the way to Pittsburgh, then Branch would see him.

A few weeks later, as McClannen walked into the Forbes Field office, Rickey explained that because of pressing business, he could spare only five minutes. Yet as he listened to the football coach, baseball business suddenly took a back seat to the business of faith. Rickey had finally found a man who wanted to change things. He wanted to take the work of God in a new direction. Here was a man who dreamed of instituting Christian programs for kids, outside the walls of church. This was just what Branch had wanted to see when he issued the challenge to the Methodist youth group during his 1938 meeting in Chicago.

The five minutes stretched to more than five hours, and in that time the old man and the young man outlined the concept, direction, and scope of an organization they called the Fellowship of Christian Athletes. As the meeting finally closed, Branch gave Don a few assignments, then picked up the phone. Rickey quickly persuaded several powerful Pittsburgh businessmen to underwrite the budget of the new organization. He then convinced four of baseball's great superstars to become charter members. With Robin Roberts, Otto Graham, Carl Erskine, and Don Moomaw on board, the FCA took off in a hurry. Within a few years tens of thousands had joined, and Rickey quietly watched, realizing that his calling into the world of baseball had not just broken the color line but also produced a new generation of young men and women who took to the field embracing the same kind of values he had tried to instill in the St. Louis Cardinals of the 1920s. His faith had been justified and his prayers had been answered. His Christian calling really had been baseball.

For the remainder of his life two things continued to drive Branch. The first was his love of baseball; he was instrumental in signing the first Latin American player to the major leagues and leading the way to the expansion of those leagues. The second was his faith; he freely gave his time to speak about his Christian convictions all across the country.

As he sought to further expand his Christian speaking, Rickey's health began to fail. In the fall of 1965 he suffered two heart attacks in seven weeks. The attacks left him almost too weak to move from room to room, yet even as death stared him in the face, he was still driven to keep on speaking about his faith. On November 13, 1965, against doctor's orders, he traveled from St. Louis to Columbia to speak at the University of Missouri Hall of Fame Banquet held at the Daniel Boone Hotel.

Using a cane, Branch slowly approached the dais. Glancing out over the hundreds who had gathered to hear his words, he paused, smiled, and in a strong voice began to tell the story of Zaccheus. He explained how deeply this man was driven to see Jesus. Too small in stature to catch a glimpse of the Son of God from the ground, Zaccheus climbed a tree.

After taking a deep breath, Rickey revealed that to really see Jesus in his own life, as well as understand him, he had to be like Zaccheus and go out on that limb. Rickey assured those gathered that if everyone had the faith to go out on a limb for God, then they could make an impact too.

He was about to move on to another point when he paused and quietly announced, "You will have to excuse me, I don't think I can continue." He would speak no more on that night or any other. Slumping into a chair, he fell into a deep coma. He died a month later on December 9, 1965.

As news of his passing swept the nation, two men probably best summed up who Branch Rickey really was. Jackie Robinson, whom Rickey had chosen not just to break baseball's color line but also to begin the process of breaking down all of society's racial barriers, said, "The thing about him was that he was always doing something for someone else. I know, because he did so much for me."

The Reverend Billy Graham added, "He was a rarity, a man's man and a Christian."

Yet perhaps it was Branch Rickey, the man who felt that God called him into baseball and used that call to tear down walls and help start an organization using sports to introduce millions to Christ, who best summed up the real meaning of his life. He told a group of young people, "It is not the honor that you take with you, but the heritage you leave behind."

6

NORMAN VINCENT PEALE

Learning to Be Positive

In 1945 Americans began to again feel a greater sense of security. The Axis powers had been beaten, the men who had fought the war were now coming home, and peace was the watchword of the day. Still, many had concerns about the future. Millions feared what the birth of an atomic age would mean to the globe. Did the bomb finally give humankind godlike power over all the world? Was the end of war also the end of innocence? Even in a victory where it appeared that right had triumphed over wrong, deep faith seemed to be in short supply, and despair about the future seemed to be everywhere.

Branch Rickey, the general manager of the Brooklyn Dodgers, was one of those who questioned how winning the war would change America. An optimist, he nevertheless feared that a directionless society might well bring out the worst in the American people and lead to moral decay. He wondered if the American dream could still take root in the souls of young and old alike. Had a depression and two world wars killed not only millions of American youth but also the optimistic passion to believe that with God's help we can make things better?

At a dinner party with famed newscaster Lowell Thomas, businessman J. C. Penney, former war hero and aviation pioneer Eddie Rickenbacker, and a few others, Rickey spoke of the need for inspirational role models. He argued that for the next generation to live up to the high standards of the past, these heroes had to be found and spotlighted. The men around him agreed that new generations of inspirational people were needed, but they wondered how to find their stories and share them with others.

These giants of society brainstormed for several hours before giving birth to an idea for a new publication whose sole editorial mission would be to spiritually inspire men and women through American success stories. Rickey, along with the others, felt that the man who would best serve to head up this venture was among them that night. The baseball guru pointed to the slightly built, bespectacled Brooklyn pastor Norman Vincent Peale as the man for the job.

There was no doubt in any of their minds that on this night God had placed Peale in their midst to again turn the spotlight on the potential of the American dream. After all, for more than a decade on his radio program and through his weekly sermons, Peale had been stressing that a person who thought positively, lived like Christ, and sought the moral high ground would find great happiness and peace. So he was already the spokesperson for the cause.

Like the others, the pastor saw the potential for this publication. He also felt there was need for a magazine of this sort. Yet, playing the role of spoiler, he pointed out that financing such a venture would not be easy. For this to succeed on a national level, it would have to have a solid financial foundation.

Peale had no more than spelled out the costs of such a venture when Rickey pulled out his checkbook. The others at the dinner party quickly followed Rickey's lead, and the idea became a reality. Each assured the pastor they were certain this magazine would work on a spiritual level. In a sense, they claimed victory before the battle had even been fought. A large part of this was due to Rickey's faith in Peale.

Branch Rickey had been drawn to Norman Vincent Peale because of the message he heard when the pastor preached. As a baseball manager, Rickey had once told his players that before they even stepped to the plate, they needed to visualize getting a hit.

He emphasized that if they did not believe in their abilities, they would likely fail. In Peale's sermons, Rickey heard that same kind of theme. To be something special, you have to believe that God made you to be something special. To do something big, you have to believe God has equipped you to do it.

What made Peale, a small man, such an inspiration? Why did Rickey and his associates say, "Norman *can* do this"?

Like Rickey, Norman Vincent Peale had been given a positive philosophy during his youth. Yet in Norman's case it would take years to finally take root in his soul. Born in 1898 in the southwestern Ohio town of Bowersville, Norman was the first son of Charles and Anna Peale. Charles was a doctor whose last act in the world of medicine was to deliver his child. He then walked away from a successful practice to pursue a calling to the ministry. This change in profession would result in his family having to give up a middle-class lifestyle and embrace the spartan existence of a Methodist clergyman. It would also result in the Peale family's becoming gypsy-like, as they constantly moved around Ohio to fill each new pastoral assignment. The latter consequence would have a dramatic effect on the personality and self-confidence of Charles and Anna's shy child. In fact, Norman grew so insecure that he ran from any opportunity to spotlight his God-given talents.

Being a preacher's kid during this time in American history was tough. For a small boy with hardly any confidence, it was almost torture. Norman stuttered, was deeply unsure of himself, and was bashful. He had difficulty making friends, and with his father constantly being reassigned to new congregations in new towns, the boy retreated more inwardly with each move. The child who in adulthood would preach the power of positive thinking was awash in negative thoughts about his own potential. It would be an elementary school teacher named George Reeves who finally presented a concept that laid the cornerstone of what would become a remarkable life.

Reeves was more than just a teacher; he was a motivator. One day he wrote on the blackboard in large letters the word *can't*. After cleaning the chalk dust from his fingers, he glanced back at his class and asked, "What shall I do now? How can we give this word a new meaning?" Sensing where the teacher was going, Norman awkwardly lifted his hand and in a quiet voice offered, "You could knock the *t* off the *can't*."

Smiling, Reeves jumped back to the board and erased that final letter. Then he turned back to Norman and proclaimed, "Let that be a lesson to you. You *can* if you think you can. And don't you ever forget it either."

Like George Reeves, Charles Peale was an advocate of strong faith producing great results. Many of his sermons centered on this aspect of Christian living. In a time when many pastors tried to "scare the hell out of their flocks" with fire-and-brimstone sermons, Peale spoke of healing fragile spirits. By nature a happy, jovial man, he felt that God wanted Christians to be awash in joy, not wallowing in doubt. As a former physician, he also believed that health, both physical and spiritual, was best served when a person had a positive outlook on themselves and their experiences. As an adult Norman would look back on his father's simple genius with a sense of great awe, but as a child the sermons were lost on him.

Finally, Charles recognized his son's insecurity in a way that few parents could. Before Norman was a teen, the elder Peale took his son aside and, as a doctor rather than a father, explained the source of the boy's feelings of inferiority and self-doubt. Then he changed his tone and added, "We can't afford treatments to cure you. But there is a doctor right here who can cure any disease of the mental and emotional life. He has a rare and amazing power to cure our unhealthy thought patterns. And he can heal the sensitive self-centeredness that lies at the root of inferiority-inadequacy feelings. Norman, are you willing to let this great doctor, Jesus Christ, treat you for that inferiority complex?"

At that moment Norman was not yet ready to turn his problems over to God. His inferiority was so great that he probably didn't feel comfortable approaching the Creator of the universe with such a seemingly small issue. Therefore he continued to hold back, hide many of his talents, and shy away from anything that would place him in the spotlight. Though a teacher had used logic and his father had presented lessons in faith, the word *can't* still had a much stronger position in Norman's life than the word *can*.

The next important lesson that came through his father's leadership concerned another pastor who had fallen into an addiction. Though his congregation did not realize it, this family friend had become a closet alcoholic. Yet rather than shun the man for his behavior, as most would have at the time, Charles took him into their home. He recognized that the man had an illness that was affecting his body and spirit. He was insecure and filled with guilt. The pastor explained the man's actions to Norman in both medical and pastoral language. "He is a sick, lost sheep, and it is my duty to help him come back to the flock."

A fascinated Norman watched from a distance as in a matter of weeks the man was transformed. He was able to regain his personal strength, refind his faith, and give up his addiction. With his newfound grace and optimism, the man's service to God actually grew in influence and power. He was happy again, and others sought him out because they could see his happiness. Norman would later explain that for the first time he saw the glory of Christianity, as well as the brotherhood of humility and love in action. The wonder and awe the boy witnessed in that healing and in the way his father helped institute it would impact the rest of his life.

Still, even with three powerful and pragmatic lessons of hope and faith, Norman could not rid himself of his own sense of inferiority. He would not speak in public and had problems even expressing his ideas to friends and family. He seemed destined to become the man no one ever noticed, just another little guy in the back of the room who never got his ideas out of his head. Yet Charles would not give up. Gently prodding, he kept trying to tear down the negative self-concept that was ruining his son's life.

Charles realized he was his son's hero. He knew the boy held him in awe. So one evening as the two sat alone in an Ohio church, he spoke words that must have stunned Norman. "Son, you have it in you to be a speaker, better than your father, but you must get yourself out of the picture. And the best way to do that is to put Jesus at the center. Always be real, son. Always be real!"

This charge should have finally convinced Norman of his potential. His hero thought he had greater promise than he did. Yet though he was surrounded by so many incredible examples of faith and enjoyed his hero's full support, he still refused to take a step in faith. A few years later when he went to college at Ohio Wesleyan, he was still the same shy kid who hid his talents from anyone in authority.

After several months of trying to teach the young man, one of his professors finally confronted Norman. "Peale," the teacher hollered out after class, "what's the matter with you? I know that you are proficient in this course. But you are so terribly shy, so embarrassed when I call upon you, that you get tongue-tied, red in the face, and your inferiority feelings stick out all over. No wonder students snicker. In the name of heaven, stop being a worm or a scared rabbit. You are a minister's son and ought to know something of our Savior Jesus Christ. Let him help you, for he will."

Filled with rage, Norman bolted from the classroom and almost vowed to leave the university. Alone, frightened, and angry, he finally bowed his head and humbly sought God's help.

"Lord Jesus. I need help and I need it now. You can change a drunk into a sober person, a thief into an honest man, a harlot into a good woman. Can't you change a poor soul like me into a normal person? Please, dear Lord, work your transformation in my life." This prayer started Norman on his task of building a brand-new life.

After graduating, Norman began work at a newspaper in Findlay, Ohio. While writing stories of city council meetings, house fires, and criminal trails, the young man was given one of the most important tools he would later use in a ministry that would touch millions. After reading one of Norman's elaborately written features, editor Grove Patterson looked him squarely in the eye and said, "The greatest literary device known to man is the period. Never write over one. And use as many as you can. Write in short, fast-paced sentences."

Norman was obviously confused. This was not the way he had been taught in school. Sensing that his young reporter didn't grasp what he had tried to explain, Patterson posed a question. "Norman, up at the university is an erudite professor, while down in the street is an uneducated but literate ditch digger. To which of them will you write? The answer is the ditch digger, because then both of them will understand what you are trying to say."

For the first time Norman grasped the key to what made his father's sermons so great. The elder Peale understood that to reach the masses with the gospel, he might think like a doctor but he had to speak as a common man. Otherwise many would not understand the heart of his message. Now that Norman finally understood this lesson, God was ready to use him in a very special way. But first the young man had to make a major step in faith.

He had a flair for writing. He knew how to tell a story and make it stick in people's minds. In the competitive newspaper business of the 1920s, it seemed sure he was on his way to great things. Yet he had no more arrived in the big market of Detroit than he felt the call to preach. Though it meant giving up his newfound security and stepping into a world where he would have to boldly speak his thoughts, he followed that call.

He was a seminary student at Boston University when he first stepped behind a pulpit of his own. The small Methodist church in Berkley, Rhode Island, found itself in the middle of a labor war. Many local citizens and church members were fighting for their lives in a dispute with a local mill. The strike had created a huge wave of bitterness that hung over the community like an autumn fog. Everywhere Norman looked, he saw dark clouds of despair. Even before he took a step inside the old building, Norman was warned that the situation was hopeless. This was a place that had lost its faith in everything, and no preacher, especially one with no experience, could make a difference.

As was common with most young pastors confronted with a situation too large to get their arms around, he fell back on his recent theological training. Over several days he produced a message filled with grandiose language and high, holy platitudes. He figured if he couldn't give them answers to their problems, he would wow them with his vast knowledge. Yet the night before the young man was to give that lofty address, his father's almost forgotten charge, buried deeply among the memories of youth, battled its way to the surface of his mind.

"Always be real, son. Always be real."

He then remembered the advice of his first newspaper editor to always give them something they all can understand.

As he stared at his message, he was overcome with the knowledge that he simply couldn't provide these people what they needed. "I can't," he whispered. Then he remembered the lesson George Reeves had given on the school blackboard. "Yes, with God's help, I can!"

Tossing away his prepared text, he opened his Bible to John 10:10: "The thief cometh not, but for to steal, and to kill, and to destroy: I am come that they might have life, and that they might have it more abundantly."

The next morning Norman didn't preach but rather spoke about the love of God. He told his new flock about Jesus healing the sick, turning sinners into good men and women, bringing out the best in boys and girls. The positive, simple message worked that day and continued to work the next Sunday and all the Sundays that followed. Within weeks the pews were overflowing with those seeking to hear the gospel of love and hope presented in a way that anyone could understand.

After graduating from Boston University, Norman rebuilt the spirit and brotherhood in several more churches, each time using his direct, simple message that faith can change lives. One of those who were deeply impressed by the slightly built man was Loretta Ruth Stafford. Ruth would become Norman's wife and partner in a mission that would quickly move to America's most dynamic city.

In 1932 the young pastor was asked to take the pulpit of one of New York City's most historic houses of worship. The Marble Collegiate Church had been a part of the city since the days of Dutch rule. Many of the city's founders had called this church their home. Yet like most relics from history, Marble Collegiate was showing its age. The facilities were in a horrible state of disrepair, the congregation had shrunk to a few hundred, and the church's collection plates were almost as empty as the pews. On top of that, if he took the position at Marble, Norman would have to leave the Methodist denomination that had been so much a part of his life to become a member of the Dutch Reformed Church. To the thirty-four-year-old man it seemed like the worst possible career move. This was an impossible job — a "career ender," his friends called it — but with his wife urging him on, Norman made the leap of faith and moved with her to Brooklyn.

In front of sparse crowds, Peale continued to deliver his simple, optimistic messages. He also made thousands of visits to homes and businesses. Yet as the months passed, his flock did not increase.

Within a year the only thing upbeat about Norman was his sermons. In truth he was a defeated man, again unsure of his value as a person and a pastor.

"You've got to change your style," his friends urged. "The Depression is killing people; they need to hear hellfire and brimstone. No one wants to hear about better times coming, because they know they aren't."

His friends were right in one way: the churches that were growing were preaching about gloom and doom. They were not giving hope, just trying to scare the lost into looking to heaven and forgetting about better times ever coming back to the sinful earth. Certainly few at his church still felt that their best days were ahead. He would later write of this time, "From the pulpit on Sundays I looked at the empty balconies and the wide, empty areas on the main floor, and had to make another decision. How could those balconies and empty spaces be filled? A sensational type of preaching might do it and quickly; and in those days of the 1930s there were such preachers. In fact, I actually saw, with my own eyes, a sermon topic advertised on a Brooklyn church: 'If I Were the Devil, What in Hell Would I Do?' But as a firm believer in the Holy Bible, I claimed the scriptural promise 'If I be lifted up … [I] will draw all men unto me' (John 12:32). My purpose must be not to fill seats but to fill souls with the gospel of the Lord Jesus Christ. This became my policy, and I preached to human need, always dealing with the definite problems of men and women in readily understandable thought and language forms. And I kept at it Sunday after Sunday."

Month after month Norman drove home his optimistic message that positive thinking is just another term for faith. As fire-and-brimstone messages lost favor, his simple sermons brought increasing numbers into his church. Soon others outside of Brooklyn began to get wind of a revival in one of the city's oldest churches.

NBC radio executives listened to the man and wondered if his optimistic message might work on the airwaves. The broadcasting team even convinced doubtful sponsors to give the pastor a try. Centered around Peale's growing list of simple platitudes such as "Nothing of great value in this life comes easily," "The things of highest value sometimes come hard," and "Start each day by affirming peaceful, contented and happy attitudes and your days will tend to be pleasant and successful," the temporary experiment worked. Peale's *Art of Living* would become a radio mainstay for more than five decades.

With the nation now hearing Norman's optimistic brand of faith, pastors began to seek him out for advice for their own sermons. Within five years of landing on the radio, the pastor was mailing out 750,000 copies of his sermons a month. In the meantime the Marble Collegiate Church had grown from a few hundred faithful to more than five thousand members. Even more important, the congregation was involved in ministry outreach that touched almost every part of New York City.

One of the most dynamic of these programs was housed in the basement of the church. Working with psychiatrist Dr. Smiley Blanton, Norman founded a mental health clinic that grew into an operation with more than twenty psychiatric doctors and psychologically trained ministers. With Peale pioneering the merger of theology and psychology, the field of Christian psychology was born. His use of psychology in counseling parishioners was three-quarters of a century ahead of the times. Within two decades his clinic would treat tens of thousands of men, women, and children and merge with the Academy of Religion and Mental Health to form the Institutes of Religion and Health.

Then on that fateful night in 1945, with war winding down and with the support of Branch Rickey, Lowell Thomas, and J. C. Penny, Norman started *Guideposts*. Though it would struggle to find a market for several years, the publication would eventually grow into the thirteenth-largest paid-circulation magazine in the nation. Yet Norman's biggest impact was yet to be felt.

In 1952 Ruth Peale found a manuscript her husband had thrown in the trash. Picking it up, she read it and was convinced the project had great value. She asked Norman to rework the first draft and send it to a publisher. Peale completed *The Power of Positive Thinking* when he was fifty-four years old.

Not fully understanding why, Norman Vincent Peale suddenly became controversial. Even as his book hit the bestseller list, he was being attacked on every front. Norman's message that everyone should fill their life with a positive faith and that faith can cure a world of ills was immediately embraced by common people. Strangely, this concept of faith in action was largely rebuked by not only deep thinkers but also many Christian leaders. The intellectuals argued that the book's concepts were too simple, while many theologians called the work "cultism" or "watered-down faith." For a while Norman feared his bestselling book would cost him his life's work and result in his becoming a negative influence in the community of faith he had worked so hard to expand. He even spoke of resigning and pulling out of the spotlight. But his father, now retired, again urged him to look back at his own faith and move forward.

As his father's words caused Norman to restudy his life, he recalled what he had long told others who had been caught in the darkness of doubt: "Through persistence, self-knowledge, prayer, commitment, optimism, a resolute trust in God, and the building of your own personal moral strength, you can enjoy the blessings of a deeper faith, and face the difficulties of life with courage and confidence."

Now, with editorials and sermons railing against his positive faith views, Norman had to live his own sermons. And he did. Not only did he survive, but soon other church voices saw the wisdom of a simple message that showed that God can empower any man or woman to great things. In time his view of faith put into action was proven by the positive results seen in millions of lives.

In his last years, Branch Rickey wrote to Norman Vincent Peale thanking him for his spiritual leadership. He ended his letter with this assessment of the pastor's life: "A visit with you is a great inspiration to me. I get younger and I want to do more and better. Our Christianity needs more hitting in the pinches. We need to know what we believe and why, and then we will have more confidence in our swing. Home runs don't count unless the bases are touched in order. I don't know of anyone who gets more players on first base than you do."

Norman died after a stroke on December 24, 1993, in Pawling, New York. He was as vital and alive at the end as he was seven decades before when he decided to live by these words: "Many people are tired simply because they are not interested in anything. Nothing ever moves them deeply. To some people it makes no difference what's going on or how things go. Their personal concerns are superior even to all crises in human history. Nothing makes any real difference to them except their own little worries, their desires, and their hates. They wear themselves out stewing around about a lot of inconsequential things that amount to nothing. So they become tired. They even become sick. The surest way not to become tired is to lose yourself in something in which you have a profound conviction."

When Norman Vincent Peale opted to lose his fears and shyness by immersing himself in faith, his life dramatically changed. When he completely embraced the lessons given to him by his father, teachers, and mentors and finally wiped the *t* away from *can't*, he was ready to accept his call. His life proved that through faith we can do anything God calls us to. His can-do attitude changed not just his life but also millions of other lives.

7

GEORGE WASHINGTON CARVER

Growing Where Planted

It was 1924 and George Washington Carver was sixty years old. Born a slave, he had overcome seemingly insurmountable obstacles time and time again. He knew presidents and kings, worked with the likes of Henry Ford and Thomas Edison, produced concepts that were dramatically changing the world of agriculture and industry, was one of the few men of his color welcomed into the homes of the rich and famous, and yet this great, ground-breaking revolutionary whose fame had circled the globe still lived in a single, meagerly furnished room. The suit he wore was old, rumpled, and even patched in a few places. His shoes were scuffed, and his bow tie leaned dramatically to the left. So when he rose in front of the Women's Board of Domestic Missions of the Reformed Church of America at New York City's famed Marble Collegiate Church, he appeared more like a humble janitor than the American genius who had been invited to provide words of great wisdom that day.

Looking out over the throng, sensing the historical elements that had fallen into place to put a black man behind the pulpit of a congregation whose roots went back to 1628, Carver could not help but think of the irony of this moment. He had come to the oldest Protestant church in America to speak of the brotherhood of Christianity, he had come to express the viewpoint given to him by his white foster mother — that all people were God's children — yet he had made that trip to New York City in a train coach designated only for members of the Negro race. Though there were tens of thousands of African-Americans within a few blocks of this ornate cathedral, the only black person at the conference was Carver himself. And that seemed to be the way it almost always was. Wherever he traveled outside of his classrooms at the Tuskegee Institute, whenever he met with the country's movers and shakers or addressed meetings or even Congressional committees, he was usually the only dark face in the room.

That is the way it had been for almost his entire life. He was the black infant with white parents, the only black among those homesteading in Kansas, the lone black at two different colleges, and now again the only black in God's house. Yet more than five decades after his foster mother told him, "George, you are one of God's most special children," he wondered why more of those children had not been given the respect accorded him. And now as he looked out at this gathering, was there anything he could say to help his audience understand that all of God's people are special?

In just a few years Norman Vincent Peale would bring his positive thinking to Marble Collegiate Church, but though Carver didn't patent the idea, those gathered now would find out that he had employed this concept throughout his entire life. It was the reason he was speaking that day and the reason the world was listening to what he had to say. He was the product and the triumph of an optimistic, living faith.

Glancing at his notes, the educator began to share some of his remarkable experiences. He spoke of the struggles he had faced, the foster family who had loved and nurtured him, the hurdles he had cleared, and the failures that had knocked him back. With each story, he emphasized the importance faith had played in meeting every new challenge. He told the audience he would not have achieved a single thing without faith. It was faith that drove him, faith that sustained him, and faith that brought him to them that day. Picking up his Bible, he added, "No books ever go into my laboratory. The thing that I am to do and the way of doing it comes to me. I never have to grope for methods. The method is revealed at the moment I am inspired to create something new. Without God to draw aside the curtain, I would be helpless."

For Carver, whose scientific notes often contained biblical references, this combination of faith and inspiration was what drove him to devote his life to unlocking the secrets of nature. He saw it as doing God's work. He felt he had been called out of slavery and through a long series of slow and painful steps to positively impact the world in this way. As he had been lifted up by the faith of his foster mother, so he now wanted to lift and inspire others.

George was born into slavery in Diamond Grove, Missouri, in 1864. At birth he was given no last name; he was simply known as Moses Carver's property. In any case, the breath of life within him was almost extinguished before he celebrated his first birthday.

During the final months of the Civil War, George, his brother James, and his mother were kidnapped. Moses Carver spent weeks wandering through the Ozark hills trying to track down the trio. By the time the German immigrant finally trailed his slaves to a farm in Arkansas, the mother had died and the children were deathly ill. Outgunned, Moses traded his three-hundred-dollar racehorse for the boys. It was a deal that made no financial sense; the horse was worth far more than George or James. But as a Christian, Moses simply couldn't abandon the orphans. He felt a responsibility for them.

The moment that Moses took George into his arms was a turning point in the man's life. Slavery suddenly disgusted him. He realized he couldn't own these children, because they were God's. Why hadn't he known it before? Why had it taken holding the child to see God in the tiny boy's eyes? From that moment forward Moses and his wife, Susan, treated the boys as if they were their own children, even giving them their last name and ignoring the racial lines that had once so profoundly divided master from slave.

The Carvers were deeply religious, and through the family devotionals George learned a great deal about the Bible. Long before he could read, he latched on to the verse "And you shall know the truth and the truth shall set you free." He was curious about what that meant. Since the Civil War had ended, he knew he was technically free—Moses had told him that time and time again—but how had that freedom changed his life? And what kind of freedom was Jesus talking about?

Freedom for the slaves had changed little. The world was still segregated, and black children were simply not welcome in the white world. Most blacks were taught that because God had made them dark in color, they would always be limited to menial work and modest dreams. Blacks were discouraged from seeking education, much less wealth.

A frail boy, George spent much of his youth doing household chores and tending gardens. Sick or not, his curiosity knew no bounds. On his own he discovered that different types of plants liked different soils, different amounts of water, and varying amounts of sunlight. He also found out you could take soaps and other household products and coat the leaves on trees to repel certain types of destructive insects. Inspired by something he heard Susan read from the Bible, he learned to graft trees. By the age of ten he had become the area's plant doctor.

Susan, after watching him tend a garden, told the boy, "George, you are special, and God has special plans for you." Although she seemed to sincerely believe this, Moses shook his head. If George had been their real son, if he had been born white, then maybe Susan's prophecy would have a chance at coming true, but it was a sad fact that the world had no place for a former slave, even one who was smart. Moses figured that God himself couldn't change that. So he was sure George was destined for a life spent in the shadows.

At the Lincoln School for Negro Children, George learned to read, write, and spell. Upon graduation he applied to several colleges. Only one, Highland College in Kansas, accepted him. He was overjoyed. With ten dollars in his pocket he walked for days to get to school by the September 13 deadline. Proudly presenting his letter of acceptance, he waited to be welcomed. Instead he was abruptly turned away. Highland had not realized till then that George was black. Thus the door of hope and opportunity closed even more quickly than it had been opened.

Over the next ten years Carver wandered the Great Plains, learning how to live off the land from Native Americans, homesteading and farming in new areas of settlements in the West, and working as a cook at hotels. For much of this time his only consistent companion was his Bible. Everything else in life was transitory. And as the years melted away, as the doors of opportunity were constantly shut in his face simply because of the color of his skin, the slightly built man lost much of his optimism. Beaten down by the cold facts of life and the segregation laws of his own country, he almost became reconciled to just existing.

Yet innate curiosity, something he could not shake, drove him slowly forward. Even though it seemed to benefit no one, he continued to study soil, plants, and animal life. He explained to those who felt he was wasting his time that knowing the mysteries of life would bring him closer to God. Thus seeing God's hand in nature might help George find God's plan for his life.

Most laughed, shook their heads, and told George that God didn't have any plans for a Negro. They urged him to be satisfied with making enough to get by, and leave dreams of changing the world to those who had been born with a lighter skin color. Yet, appreciated or not, George continued to study every facet of the world around him. His faith assured him that what he was learning would somehow be used down the road. But how long was that road?

In 1890 George's wanderings led him to Indianola, Iowa. Shyly he inquired if Simpson College allowed Negro students. He found out that though they had no blacks at the time, one member of his race had gained an education at Simpson many years before. If he could pass the entrance requirements and find a job to pay his own way, he would be welcome to attend classes on the small campus. Overcome with joy, George finally found himself in the place he had wanted to be since leaving Missouri.

George excelled in art and music and was quickly recognized as the school's star student. But an instructor, Etta Budd, felt Carver's real talents were being wasted. He was much brighter than anyone she had ever met, and his knowledge of plants was beyond anything she had ever seen. She told him, "George, you are special. God has special plans for you." Yet unlike Susan Carver, who could not offer any insight into those plans, Etta Budd presented a road map to her prize pupil. Etta's father was the head of the Iowa State College Department of Horticulture. After meeting George, Joseph Budd won a spot for George at Iowa State. In 1891 the former slave became the historic school's first African-American student. Yet he quickly found out he was still considered a second-rate citizen.

Carver was given a mattress and forced to sleep in an unused room in the administration building. He was not allowed to eat meals in the dining hall. Many of the other students would not even acknowledge his presence, much less speak to him. As he fought through the lonely times, Susan Carver's belief in him came through in her letters and kept him from giving up.

Professor Joseph Budd found ways to spotlight Carver's vast knowledge of horticulture. Thanks to Budd's putting George's work on display, other students struggling with their studies quietly sought out the black man for tutoring. In a few months his intelligence, kindness, and smile won them over. The students invited him to eat with them, sleep in the dorms, and be a part of their organizations. He became a trainer for the athletic teams, captain of the campus military regiment, student head of the agricultural department, writer for the student newspaper, and had two paintings win awards at the 1893 World's Fair in Chicago. When he graduated with honors in 1894, he was even given a scholar-ship for graduate studies and became the state's first black college instructor.

Over the next two years, George quickly developed dynamic scientific skills in plant pathology and mycology. His advances in these fields were published by some of the top scientific periodicals. In 1897 Carver completed his master's degree and was made a full-time member of the Iowa State faculty. He was happy, content, and convinced that by using the university's wealth of facilities, he could pursue research that would prove beneficial to America's farmers. Yet a single letter knocked a hole in Carver's secure world.

Booker T. Washington, the nation's most noted African-American educator, asked George to come to Alabama's Tuskegee Institute and head up the school's agricultural department. Washington's correspondence promised little.

"I cannot offer you money, position, or fame. The first two you have. The last from the position you now occupy you will no doubt achieve. These things I now ask you to give up. I offer you in their place: work—hard, hard work, the task of bringing a people from degradation, poverty, and waste to full manhood. Your department exists only on paper and your laboratory will have to be in your head."

Carver didn't want to go. He was happy where he was; he enjoyed being in a world where he was treated as an equal because of his knowledge and proven value. As far as he was concerned, the South offered no potential for a black man. So going there for a job would be like taking a giant step backward.

Yet as he reread the letter, logic took a back seat to faith. He had been told he was special by several men and women, going back to his foster parents. These people had been there to help him realize his God-given talents. He thought back to that verse he had learned so long ago: "And you shall know the truth and the truth shall set you free." The sons and daughters of former slaves were free, but not to dream, only to exist. Society was holding them back. No one was telling them they could realize the American dream. No one had faith in their talents or was encouraging their curiosity. Their world was filled with negatives, barriers, and prejudice.

Even though his own personal battles seemed to have been won, Carver wondered if God was pushing him to inspire a new generation who had as little as he once did. So though all worldly logic told him it was the wrong thing to do, he accepted the offer to teach at Tuskegee.

Using items from dumping grounds and trash heaps, Carver created lab instruments. He then reclaimed part of a swamp for an agricultural testing plot. Working with students who were not eager to get their hands dirty, he attempted to show them the riches that could be found in God's dirt. As the methods he had learned first from Moses Carver, then from American Indians, and finally from his education in Iowa took root, young men began to grasp the potential for a life in agriculture. In Carver's weekly Bible study sessions, these same students also began to believe that God saw them as special wonders of his creation.

Carver often used the experiences in the field as a tool to enrich the spiritual growth of his charges. He would point out all that could be done with a lowly peanut plant. This bush, whose fruit grew in the soil, not only offered something to feed livestock, but it actually enriched the soil where it was planted. He then showed his students some of the things he could do with peanuts, such as making oil, flour, and even glue. Finally, after they had been sufficiently awed by the possibilities afforded this plant, he pointed out that a human being was the ultimate in God's creation. His potential was far beyond that of the peanut plant. He could not only bear great fruit but also enrich the world around him. But that could happen only if each individual chose to turn his potential over to the Lord, and his life over to those in need around him.

Using what he learned from growing peanuts and sweet potatoes, Carver developed a crop rotation that revolutionized agriculture. Expanding his goal along with his research, he sought to help "the man farthest down." He vowed to better the life of the poorest farmers by developing new farming methods and crops that would produce new markets. He composed, printed, and gave away simply written brochures that included information on every facet of farming. He also provided a free analysis of soil and water.

To take his vision to the world, he put a laboratory in a wagon and began to tour the South, sharing his ideas with blacks and whites alike. While others sold ideas, he gave them away. Why? He explained that he had once been a slave; he had once been what Christ had called "the least of these." So when God had given him the knowledge to unlock a few of nature's mysteries, it was his Christian responsibility to share this news with others rather than profit from his discoveries.

Over his first decade of teaching he redefined farming in the South as he developed thousands of products farmers could produce from both crops and soil. While realizing and proving the value of the peanut was what gained him his first bit of international fame, his work with soybeans, sweet potatoes, corn, and even livestock led to thousands of new discoveries that revolutionized agriculture in every part of the globe. Remarkably, he accomplished all this from a lab more modest than those found at most Midwestern high schools today.

By 1905 George Washington Carver was a household name, not just in his own country but also in Europe, Russia, and Japan. Daily he received letters from all over the globe. Yet it was one letter sent from a farm in Missouri that touched him most deeply. Moses Carver, now ninety-six years old, wrote his foster son telling him just how proud he was that George had become the special person Susan was sure he would become. Overcome with a sense of humble joy, the teacher boarded a train to reunite with the man who had raised him decades before.

As they relived old times, the old man noted, "I made a good deal." George was puzzled by the remark. Moses explained that his prize racehorse had not just purchased two boys' freedom; it had given the world one of the most remarkable men God had ever made. Four years later Moses died, and his eulogy listed an Alabama professor as his only remaining son. Moses' transformation from slave owner to proud parent of a free son had become complete.

By the 1920s Carver's Tuskegee lab was a destination point for everyone from the United States Secretary of Agriculture to Thomas Edison. Leaders from all over the world came to listen to his advice. Carver also had common, everyday farmers, both white and black, ride hundreds of miles just to thank him in person. The ever modest teacher would advise each visitor to thank the one who really created the miracles.

Thanks to his discoveries, Carver had become a media darling. He knew that editors and reporters saw him as either a novelty, a distraction, an enemy, or a cause. He was a novelty because he was a respected black scientist in a world where most of his race worked menial jobs and were given no respect. He was a distraction because he was an African-American who upset people's views of the division of the races. He was an enemy to many because he was welcomed into parts of society reserved for whites and thus seemed to be breaking down racial barriers. And he was a cause to those who wanted to push for the integration of America as quickly as possible.

Therefore because so much rode on everything he said and did, Carver was prodded to become more for his race and to speak in a more assertive tone. Thousands, both black and white, begged him to make the big statement, to leave his humble job in the South, to dress as a gentleman and take a position with Henry Ford or

Thomas Edison. Yet he scoffed at those who said that by changing little things about himself, he would change all of society.

"It is not the style of clothes one wears," he constantly explained, "neither the kind of automobile one drives, nor the amount of money one has in the bank, that counts. These mean nothing. It is simply service that measures success."

When asked to sum up his life, Carver answered with these words: "There are times when I am surely tried and compelled to hide away with Jesus for strength to overcome. God alone knows what I have suffered, in trying to do as best I could the job he has given me in trust to do. Most of the time I had to work without sympathy or support of those with whom I associated. Many are the strange paths God led me into.... God has so willed it that there were always a few good friends to encourage me and strengthen me when the burden seemed greater than I could bear."

In January 1943 the world was at war, but a former slave who had become an international icon was at peace. In his modest room at Tuskegee, George Washington Carver died, and millions mourned. Against all odds he had proven he was one of God's special people, not just because he climbed out of slavery to world fame but also because he then reached back down into the depths to lift so many others up to join him. Even today, six decades after his death, Carver's faith and work are still being felt by the "least of these" all over the globe.

8

WILLIAM CAREY

Birthing a Movement

At the age of thirty William Carey had no doubt he was an instrument destined to be used by God. He was as sure of that as he was that the sun would rise each morning. For a decade he had preached the Word from the pulpit, spoken of the Lord's grace to his friends and family, and studied the Bible in several different languages. He was respected and loved, his advice was sought by both believer and unbeliever, and though poor, he should have been fulfilled. Yet for reasons he did not understand, he believed he was wasting his life and God's call.

He had experienced those same emotions in Paulerspury, the English town of his birth, and in Hackleton, where he learned a trade and married his wife. Now, even in Moulton, where he had lived and worked for five years, Carey considered himself a stranger in a strange land.

Thus as he walked the streets of his community, as he held his children, and as he spoke with his wife, he did not feel at home. This world, the one he had grown up in, the one where everyone spoke the same language, the one whose culture he understood in the most minute detail, was a very troubling place. Why?

Understanding and direction were what Carey wanted and needed, and when he could not find either in his daily routine, he turned to books. He had been a curious child, the son of a man who encouraged William to ask questions and seek answers. In the mid-1700s college was reserved only for the elite members of society; thus as a teen Carey had to turn to books and self-study.

Though curious about science, Carey found that his greatest talents were in language. He effortlessly picked up the meanings and nuances of foreign languages. He could study Latin or Spanish for a few months and then read the most complex novels in those languages. He picked up Greek and Hebrew as easily as many learn to mend a shirt or raise a garden. His gift was so unusual and dynamic, it should have paved the way to a successful career in international business or diplomacy. Yet because he was the son of a weaver, Carey's talent was of little use. In England of this period men were born to power; they rarely earned it with their accomplishments or God-given and work-honed skills. Thus when he should have gone on to higher education, Carey trained as a shoemaker.

Beyond laboring at his regular job as a cobbler, Carey also preached at a small church. Yet because that job paid for little more than his study materials, he spent over sixty hours each week working with other people's shoes. As he toiled, stretching leather around soles, he occupied his mind by studying a crude map he had drawn and tacked on a far wall. With each new day, the map begged Carey to leave England and explore the world.

During his lunch hour, Carey often escaped his small and demanding world by picking up a book written by Scottish explorer James Cook. In thirty years, this great hero had taken his ships around the globe several times. With only his wits and courage guiding him, Cook had explored regions never visited by Europeans. He had opened up the sea for shipping and expanded the English view of the world. His books and journals had thrilled thousands, and his examples of heroic discovery had every boy in Britain dreaming of a life at sea.

Yet even after reading of Cook's adventures, the cobbler had no desire to claim new lands for the crown. So why was he so fascinated by Cook's experiences? Why had God given him a facility for languages? What could he do with his knowledge of the Pacific or with his ability to speak in five or six different tongues? All of this information was of no use to a simple shoemaker and clergyman.

In late May 1792 Carey was preparing a sermon. Because a number of Baptist ministers would be in the audience, he spent many more hours than usual on this message. After considerable contemplation, he finally chose Isaiah 54:2–3 as his text: "Enlarge the place of thy tent, and let them stretch forth the curtains of thine habitations: spare not, lengthen thy cords, and strengthen thy stakes; For thou shalt break forth on the right hand and on the left; and thy seed shall inherit the Gentiles, and make the desolate cities to be inhabited."

As he prepared his sermon, the preacher studied his hand-drawn map. Maybe the map was a sign — a message from the Lord. Perhaps he was meant to live the words of the Great Commission: "Go ye therefore, and teach all nations, baptizing them in the name of the Father, and of the Son, and of the Holy Ghost." It wasn't just England, it wasn't just Europe — Jesus was talking about the whole world.

As Carey looked back at the map, words and verses of Scripture flooded his mind at such a rapid rate that he could barely comprehend them. It was as if a dozen voices were speaking in his head at the same time. "God so loved the world! Go ye into all the world! The kingdoms of the world shall become the kingdoms of our God and of his Christ!"

It was always the world, the world. And the voices would not let him forget it. They spoke to him for hours. He couldn't escape them. Everywhere he looked, he was reminded of the world.

On May 31, 1792, with the whole world and Christ's charge to his disciples still on his mind, Carey preached in Nottingham, England. Though he wouldn't have dared forecast it, his words and the actions that followed would change the face of Christianity around the globe more than Cook's voyages had changed the United Kingdom.

"Lengthen thy cords, and strengthen thy stakes," Carey demanded of his audience that day, "for thou shalt break forth on the right hand and on the left; and thy seed shall inherit the Gentiles, and make the desolate cities to be inhabited." He presented a deep and meaningful sermon, expounding on the passage from Isaiah and paying high tribute to the Great Commission, Christ's last words on earth.

Yet as he finished, no one cried, no one came forward, and few seemed even to digest the meaning of his message. Incensed, the usually mild-mannered cobbler roared, "Are we not going to do anything?"

By the time Carey issued his challenge, most of those gathered that day had gotten up and headed to the door. Then, as the preacher's forceful words rattled the windows, they turned as one to see what had so consumed the man. As the shocked throng stared, Carey raised his hand and sobbed, "I will go. Send me!"

What is he thinking? they wondered. If God wants to save the men and women in Africa or Asia, he doesn't need Englishmen to do it. He will handle that on his own. In their minds, when Jesus spoke of saving the world, it was not that massive world James Cook visited but rather the limited world they saw in their daily routines. Carey needed to meet the needs of this area, not try to save souls in foreign lands where no one could even speak English.

As the meeting continued, those who grudgingly came back presented another very good argument against what Carey seemed to be proposing. This man who wanted to save the world was a cobbler. He had no money, no prospects, and he had never been overseas. All he had was a vision, and what good was that? "So," they demanded to know, "how can an uneducated cobbler go to a strange land and reach uncaring heathens?"

Carey forcefully answered, "If you have enough faith, everything is possible."

Probably as much to soothe Carey's angry spirit as to commit to supporting a missionary movement, those gathered passed the following resolution: "Resolved, that a plan be prepared against the next ministers' meeting at Kettering, for forming a Baptist Society for propagating the Gospel among the Heathens."

True to this mission statement, several months later the Baptist Missionary Society was organized. The group then raised thirty pounds designated to "save the world's people." Carey was so thrilled that he was immediately ready to pack his bags and live out the Great Commission. Yet few of the other members of the society believed that the cobbler would ever leave his shop, much less England.

Burning with a fire to leave England and evangelize the world, Carey knew he had found his calling. He was ready to be the James Cook of Christianity. Yet even if he was ready to take a huge leap in faith, he had to have someplace to land. So the question became, where would he start? As he studied his homemade map, he was overwhelmed by having to choose a place to go. He might have remained confused if not for an English preacher who had recently spent time in India. John Thomas convinced the cobbler that India was where the work of spreading the gospel needed to start. With all the British influence now in this nation, the people had to be ready to hear the good news. Now Carey had not only a call but also a destination that seemed suited for his talents.

A master of five European tongues, Carey was convinced that within a few months he could master the Indian dialects and lead thousands to salvation just through his preaching. With that as a foundation, he could then start a movement that would bring the entire nation to Christianity. To the cobbler it was just that simple.

The government of England, along with the established Anglican Church, was not nearly as enthusiastic as Carey. They viewed the cobbler as an uneducated rabble-rouser. The business world feared that the missionary would stir people up and create a climate of revolution. Carey's most powerful opponent was the largest and most influential economic power of the time, the East India Company. Thanks in large part to this group's lobbying of the Crown and the House of Commons, Carey was refused the necessary papers to leave England.

Struck down before he could even begin, a frustrated Carey restudied his homemade map. He felt sure God wanted him in India, but if this was so, why were there so many roadblocks in his way? The cobbler became even more frustrated when his wife joined the chorus demanding they stay in England.

Dorothy was the exact opposite of her husband. Where he was outgoing, she was shy. Where he was a voracious reader, she could not even write her own name. Where he sought adventure, she sought quiet. Where he had courage, she trembled at the sight of a mouse. As she pointed to their young children, she declared again and again, "I will not go and neither will the boys."

As government, business, the established church, and even his family rose up against him, the cobbler reread Andrew Fuller's pamphlet "The Gospel Worthy of All Acceptance." Fuller's charge had been for all men to accept responsibility for spreading the hope of salvation. These words had become the backbone of the Baptist movement and what set the upstart denomination apart from the other emerging Christian groups.

Carey had to look no farther than the life of the disciples to see the sacrifices and rewards of giving everything for faith. These men were his role models, and though most of them had died horrible deaths for their beliefs, their lives had established the faith all across the known world. Now the world was expanding, and it was time for Christianity to once again spread the faith. So even though the government wouldn't open the door, even though the most powerful business force in the Far East stood against him, even though the church opposed him, and even though his wife would not support him, he would not be denied.

Unable to get the permission of his own government to enter India, on June 13, 1793, thirty-one-year-old Carey opted to skirt the laws of Britain by boarding a Dutch sailing ship headed to the Far East. The cobbler was overjoyed as he left his native land behind, but his elation would quickly be dampened.

Storms plagued the journey. A trip that should have been easy became a Job-like experience. Dorothy's mind broke during the long periods without seeing land. She often spent days in their small cabin screaming. By November, when the family finally arrived in Calcutta, she was hopelessly insane. Carey assumed that being on dry ground and seeing the positive results of his missionary efforts would heal her fragile mind. He was wrong. She was never well again.

As hard as it had been just to get to India, Carey quickly discovered that making a beachhead for Christ in this strange land would be much more difficult. Even if he could have spoken in a language the Indian people understood, no one wanted to listen to him. Within two months he was out of funds, had made no inroads in his mission, and found his wife even more paranoid than she had been during the journey.

It was a sad, depressed Carey who wrote his friends in England asking for help. Few of his letters were answered, and those who did write back offered little financial or spiritual aid. In fact, some people argued that his struggles proved that if God wanted to save the people of India, he would do it himself. They further argued that the missionary should give up his dream and return to his work as a cobbler.

Yet, thinking of the trials of Paul, Carey would not give up. If the people of Calcutta would not listen to him, he would take the message out into the rural areas. But even in those remote places, few understood what he was saying, and those who did know

English waved him off. He was a foreigner, and he was not to be trusted. This realization gave Carey the perfect excuse to quit. Yet rather than turn his back on a calling, he spent the next several months studying the Bengali language. When he felt his knowledge was such that he could fully explain the faith in this tongue, he went back to his one-on-one ministry. Though he was now better received, he was again rebuffed when he asked the Indian people to accept Christ.

With Dorothy's condition growing worse, with her wild ravings frightening everyone she met, Carey was at the end of his rope. He seemed worthless as both a husband and a missionary. Maybe Dorothy had been correct; maybe they should not have left England. Why had he made this step in faith? Why had he come to India?

Carey couldn't go home; he didn't have the money for boat fare. His dream shattered, the humbled missionary took a job as the manager of an indigo factory. Moving to Manbatty, the former cobbler spent his days overseeing the dye-creating operations, and his nights translating the New Testament into Bengalese.

In 1797, more than four years after arriving in India in hopes of quickly converting millions to Christianity, Carey finally won over his first convert. Ironically, it wasn't an Indian; it was a man who had moved to the Far East from Portugal. Inspired by this modest success, the missionary built a small church. Yet no one came forward, and Carey's lack of converts caused even his strongest supporters in England to write him off as a failure. Using the excuse that he was now employed in the secular world, the missionary society ended all support. Carey now lived in a world that wouldn't listen to him, having been completely cut off from a world where people thought him either a charlatan or a fool. As he listened to his wife's screams, Carey began to believe that Job had had it easy.

On Sundays Carey held services for his workers, even speaking in their language, but no one responded. Each day he opened the church, but no one came. As the months became years, he grew more and more convinced he was a failure as a husband, father, and missionary. Did God call him, or did Carey invent that call? Just when he was sure he had fallen as far as he could, a flood wiped out the factory he managed, a son died, and his wife sank even further into insanity. He even began to wonder if he were not as crazy as she was.

In 1799, with no resources and no direction, a discouraged Carey moved to Serampore. The local government administrator offered Carey a home and a job as a schoolmaster. The missionary was also given access to a print shop. The press would finally give Carey his first bit of success as a missionary.

After translating the Bible and printing it in Bengalese, Carey once again attempted one-on-one evangelism. One of the thousands who heard the missionary's message was Krishna Pal. Carey also gave Pal one of his newly printed Bibles. The combination of hearing Carey speak of God's love and reading the Bible in the local tongue produced an awakening in Pal's soul. Now, seven long years after Carey first set foot in India, his work finally produced a native convert.

Over the next four years, even though only a handful of men and women followed Pal, Carey set about translating the Bible into several other Indian dialects, including Hindustani and Sanskrit. With Bibles in hand, he even opened up new missionary outposts in the communities around Serampore. Yet when measured in souls saved, his work was still a failure. It seemed he had given his life to a cause that would produce little fruit. Still, while the Bibles he distributed were having minimal impact in the Indian community, they played a part in saving the cobbler from living the remainder of his life in obscurity.

Due to his knowledge of Indian languages, proven by his biblical translations, the English community in India, which until this time had ignored Carey, sought him out to teach Sanskrit, Bengali, and Marathi to English business students at Williams College, Calcutta. Paid more than 1,200 pounds a month, Carey could now live in relative luxury. Yet though he was a professor by trade, he was still a missionary at heart. So he used less than ten percent of his income for himself and his family and spent the remainder creating more Bibles for the people of India.

In 1807 Dorothy died. Though he mourned her passing, his wife's death allowed Carey to be much more mobile. When he wasn't teaching, he was on the road preaching. In the past only a few had come to listen to him, but now thousands were drawn by curiosity about a white man who spoke so many different Indian languages. Still, no matter what tongue he employed, few accepted his message of hope and salvation. He was beating his head against a wall that would not budge.

While on one of his trips, Carey witnessed the burning of a widow at her husband's funeral. He was shocked and appalled. He begged those forcing the healthy elderly woman onto the fire to let her live. They pushed him back and cheered as her body was consumed by flames. Why had this happened? What had possessed these people to kill this poor woman?

As he toured his adopted nation, the missionary watched this horrible tradition, called suttee, play out again and again. Since only a handful of Indian people had accepted faith through his preaching, Carey wondered if God had led him to India to stop the barbaric practice of human sacrifice. He now knew he couldn't rest without at least attempting to stop the suttee. This would become even more important to him than establishing new congregations.

In 1829, more than thirty-eight years after setting foot in Calcutta, Carey had distributed thousands of Bibles and preached countless sermons but had only a few converts to show for his work.

Yet while many looked at him as a failure, the old man who had stubbornly refused to give up on reaching the lost in India finally had reason to celebrate. The government had outlawed suttee. He was preparing for church on that Sunday morning when the news of the ruling reached him. A smile framing his face, he exclaimed, "No church for me today; if I delay an hour to translate and publish this, many a widow's life may be sacrificed."

Quickly newspapers throughout the world told of how the missionary had changed the mindset of the Indian people and in the process saved millions of innocent lives. Three decades after being dismissed as a failure, suddenly the Englishman who had stopped the suttee was finally seen as a Christian lion! Ironically, saving the lives of widows also opened up a new curiosity in India. What had so driven this man to rescue old women he did not know? Thousands who had once ignored Carey now asked to read one of the Bibles he had printed.

In 1833, though he was again enthused about his spiritual work, Carey was physically broken and weak. At seventy-two, he had finally seen his faith realized in a measurable way, but he was too ill to take advantage of the door that had opened. Because of Carey's Job-like testimony and the publicity created by his crusade against the suttee, thousands in England were boarding boats armed with the faith to follow in his footsteps. Those who once ridiculed him were now calling him a giant and pointing to his methods of learning the language and the culture as the only way to win souls in a foreign land. Though he had known much more failure than success, he had created the mold for all missionaries to follow, and thousands wanted to walk in the cobbler's shoes.

"There is nothing remarkable in what I have done," he told a friend. "It has only required patience and perseverance.... When I compare things as they now are in India with what they were when I came here, I see that a great work has been accomplished, but how it has been accomplished, I know not."

In June 1834 Alexander Duff came to visit. Duff was one of those young men so inspired by Carey's work that he had come to India to be a missionary. During his visit the Scotsman spent hours praising the old man and speaking of how he was one of the world's greatest heroes of faith.

Finally, after listening to Duff rave about him for more than an hour, a weary Carey lifted his hand. "Mr. Duff, you have been speaking about Dr. Carey, Dr. Carey, Dr. Carey! When I am gone, please say nothing about Dr. Carey—speak only of Dr. Carey's Savior."

Carey came to India to save millions, but he actually led only a handful to Christ with his words. When he lost the support of his friends in England, when his family suffered tragedy, when he failed to gain converts, he did not give up on his calling. Rather than admit failure, he sought a new way to reach the lost of India. Using his language skills, he translated the Bible into scores of Indian languages and dialects. It was this behind-the-scenes effort that opened India to missionary work. It also set the pattern for the Bible to become the most translated and published book in the world.

A historian once noted this about the man who personally led so very few to Christ: "Taking his life as a whole, it is not too much to say that he was the greatest and most versatile Christian missionary sent out in modern times."

Today, so many years after he died, William Carey's mantra "Expect great things from God and do great things for God" is embraced by hundreds of thousands of missionaries all over the globe. Even though few now remember his name or his story, his influence remains strong, as he defined the method still used in foreign missions work. Though few suffer such oppression and isolation, and though few now work so long with no results, modern missionaries are very much following the path blazed by the first missionary to India. In almost every case, those following in the cobbler's footsteps usually discover the knowledge, understanding, and hope found in doing the Lord's work and following the call of faith.

9

JOHN DOUGLAS
Beginning Anew

It was 1957, and John Douglas was fifty-two years old. He was tired, hungry, and sweating in the humid air that clung to him like a warm blanket. As the choir sang in a tongue he did not understand, he wiped his brow and waited to see if anyone in the crowd of several hundred would respond to his message. And as he studied the throng that night, he questioned if they understood any more of his words than he did the lyrics of the invitation hymn. "Dear Lord," he silently prayed, "please allow at least one to come forward." Yet no one moved. In fact, they seemed to stare right through him with dark, uncaring eyes.

Douglas had given his message that evening in English. After each sentence, he had been forced to stop and wait until his remarks were translated into several different languages. So while the surroundings had in many ways been familiar, the event was as foreign to him as the nation he was visiting.

It had seemed so easy when he packed for the trip. He figured he would deliver one of his old evangelical sermons, and because God's message was always the same, people would understand and come forward in large numbers as they had in West Virginia, Kentucky, and Tennessee. Yet as he stood by himself on the platform, he now knew that the only two things that leading a crusade in India had in common with his days of traveling the United States were the message and the tent. Everything else seemed very different indeed.

He had told a friend that going to India would be like walking in the footsteps of the great British missionary William Carey.

What Douglas hadn't figured was that his efforts would produce the same kind of limited success as had Carey's sermons. It was wearisome and depressing, to say the least.

As insects hovered around the three-hundred-watt bulb suspended above his head, Douglas continued to study the crowd. Only a few were singing and just a handful were praying. For the moment it seemed his message from Matthew 25 had not gotten through to any minds or hearts. Had he traveled halfway around the globe, made his way across the Indian landscape by train, antique car, and oxcart only to waste his time speaking words no one wanted to hear?

Now, feeling so alone, he realized how much he missed his family, waiting at home in West Virginia. If only he could be there tonight, sharing a good meal, hearing about their lives, and maybe listening to a favorite radio program. At least this horrid experience would soon be ending. There was some comfort in knowing that he would be with them within the week. And when he did leave India, Douglas felt sure it would be the final time he would ever see this land or visit with its people. He was old enough and wise enough to know when and where God needed him, and this was apparently not the time or the place.

In the back of the room, movement caught his eye. Maybe the trip had not been completely in vain. Someone was getting up. It was a man, well dressed in typical India garb, his dark eyes alive with energy, an almost wicked smile framing his face. Had he heard the Word? Had he been touched by the message? It was everything the preacher could do not to leap off the podium and race to meet the stranger.

As the man made his way to the aisle, Douglas noted that seven children were following him. They were dressed in little more than rags; the oldest could not have been more than ten, the youngest just a toddler. They were obviously confused, frightened, and hungry. They looked more dead than alive, and they clung to each other as if shell-shocked. As they grew closer to Douglas, the minister was so caught up in the children's horrible condition that he almost didn't hear the man pose a simple question in English.

"Do you believe what you said tonight?"

Glancing into the man's sinister eyes, Douglas nodded. "I believe every word."

"Then," the man continued, "do you live the words you speak?"

"I do my best to follow Christ's teaching," the American assured him.

"I am a Hindu," the man continued. "I have listened to you tonight, and I brought these seven with me to hear you. Your words are beautiful, the message you speak is powerful, but now I want to see if you actually feel strongly enough about what you said to live your words."

Douglas looked from the man back to the children. For the moment, these eight people were the only ones he noted. It was as if the rest of the crowd, and even the world, had disappeared.

"Preacher," the Hindu man continued, "these children's parents were recently killed in a political dispute. These seven have no one who will take care of them. They have no clothes, no food, no home, and certainly no money. Tonight you said that we need to feed the hungry, clothe the naked, and care for those who have nothing. Here are seven who are, how did you say it, 'the least of these.' Will you take care of them? Will you live the words you asked us to live? Their parents died for what they believed; will you live for what you say you believe?"

Douglas pushed his dark-rimmed glasses up on his nose and took a long look at the frightened children who stood before him. How could he take care of them? He was due to leave for home in a few days. His tour of India was over. He couldn't take them to America. There was simply no logical way that he could do anything for them. Yet what would happen if he left them here? What would happen if he just walked away? They would surely die. And how could he live with himself if he did not meet the Hindu man's challenge by living his own message?

"What do you expect me to do?" Douglas asked.

"Feed, clothe, and care for them," came the direct reply.

Douglas had come to India to preach, not be a nanny. Yet as if he were looking into the face of God, the American nodded. "I will do so."

The Indian man said something to the children and walked off. In unison the seven little ones stared at Douglas, completely unsure of their fate. Stepping toward them, he reached out his arms and embraced each. Even as he spoke comforting words, he wondered how he was going to care for children who didn't understand a single thing he said. What he did know was that these children were the reason he had been called to India.

That first night the seven stayed with Douglas in his hotel room. The next day he went out into the city, with the seven following along like ducklings, to find a home he could rent. Securing a modest house, he paid for a few months' rent and moved in with his new family.

The evangelist then sought help from the local Christian community. A pastor put him in touch with a compassionate woman who needed work. Douglas hired her as a full-time governess, set up a bank account to provide clothing, food, and school supplies for the children, and stayed in India long enough to make sure things were running well. When he was convinced that the children were in good hands, he returned to the States, but not before vowing to the little ones that he would soon return to them.

On his way back to the airport, the minister noted scores of other children living on the streets. They looked much like the ones he had rescued. Digging through trash, dressed in rags, sleeping in alleyways, they all appeared sick and hopeless. In some places he even noted children who had died, their bodies simply lying in the street waiting for a trash collector to throw them away. Why had he not seen all this before? And why was God showing it to him now? What could a poor preacher do for so many needy third world orphans?

The images of starving, homeless children haunted Douglas as he took the long series of flights from Bombay to England and on to the United States. The Hindu man's question, "Will you live the words you asked us to live?" followed him too, constantly taunting him, demanding even more than just reaching out to seven children, always pushing him to reveal the depths of his faith. How had the small-town preacher gotten himself into such a situation? How was he going to meet the demands of taking care of an orphaned family of frightened kids whose language he did not know? Until this moment he had believed that his life experiences had been so wide that he was prepared for anything, but now as he looked back over five decades, he wondered if anything he had done could help him fulfill his new commitment.

John E. Douglas was born in West Virginia in 1905. The son of a deeply devoted Christian businessman, he had been active in church since childhood. Even as a small child, he had sensed that God had called him to do something. Before he was a teen, he had gotten up early on Sunday mornings to start the fire in the stove that heated their country church. He had also rung the bell announcing the beginning of each service. These were jobs he didn't take lightly, but he hardly saw them as anything more than duties. And when church elders told him they thought he should surrender his life to preach, he knew they were wrong. He would teach Sunday school and sing in the choir, but he was sure his calling was in business. So after high school he went to work for a local store.

Within a few years Douglas would buy that business and open a number of other successful department stores throughout the South. Now married and blessed with two children, he enjoyed a nice home, fine clothes, and top-of-the-line cars. He was so good at his work that even during the Depression, when many stores were failing, he found himself becoming wealthy.

Yet at the very time when he should have been satisfied, he found himself longing for more. He soon discovered it wasn't money that lured him; it was making a difference in the world. So maybe the elders had been right. He had remained active in church, always tithing and even speaking from the pulpit at special services; maybe he had gotten a call and ignored it.

Looking for answers, Douglas sold his businesses, committed to a life as a clergyman, and plunged into pastoring rural churches throughout the South. His dynamic sermons and outgoing personality helped his churches to flourish and made him a star in his denomination. He eventually filled several different regional national offices and in his spare time earned the title of doctor of divinity.

Yet though he was respected, revered, and loved, he still was not satisfied. He felt that God needed him to do more and that he was again somehow ignoring a call. But what more was there to accomplish? He had given up his successful life in business, he had built churches and become a leader in his denomination, and he had even toured the nation leading highly successful revival meetings. What else could he do?

An English missionary, Reginald Courts, told John of his travels to India. Courts assured him that people were hungry for the power of Jesus there. They had even asked Courts to find Christian leaders who would come to India. At the time, this was not the kind of invitation Douglas had prayed to receive, so he ignored it.

First as a businessman and later as a pastor, Douglas had spent much of his life on the road. He had hated those long weeks when he was separated from his family. When he had worked revival meetings, his longing for the company of his wife and family had caused him many sleepless nights. Traveling around the globe was not on the list of things he planned to do. Besides, he was now past fifty; surely it was time for slowing down and cutting back. He was positive that the adventures of evangelizing in the third world needed to be tackled by men far younger than he. Yet even as he presented his logical arguments, Courts wouldn't let up and neither would God. For months India haunted him.

Douglas could sometimes escape the call during the day when he was working at church, but in his sleepless hours he felt God's hand pushing him toward India. There was a voice he couldn't escape telling him he was needed there. But why? There were better speakers than he within a stone's throw of his West Virginia home. In his own denomination there were scores of American preachers who spoke the tongues and understood the customs of the Indian people. He knew thousands who needed to go on this trip far more than he did. And yet in 1956, still not understanding why, Douglas went to India. But even after speaking and seeing a number saved through his messages, he didn't fully understand why he had come to this poor nation until he was challenged by the Hindu man.

Returning to the United States, Douglas began speaking to his many friends about his unique experience in India. He explained that he needed help caring for the children he had accepted as his own. As he told his story, several joined his team by pledging a few dollars each month for the care of the seven. As soon as he had secured enough funding for the first group of kids, his mind turned to the many others he had noted roaming the alleys of India. He could see their faces and hear their cries. These images haunted him so that he couldn't sleep, knowing they were dying in need of something as simple as three meals a day and a safe place to lay their heads at night.

Falling back on his business experience, Douglas formed a nonprofit organization to expand orphan care beyond those initial seven children. In 1957, with the backing of just a handful of people, World Missionary Evangelism was founded, with Douglas establishing a headquarters in Dallas, Texas. Leaving his wife and daughter in charge of the fledging ministry's day-to-day operations, he returned to India with two goals in mind. The first was to make sure that the seven children were being well provided for and that they were receiving an education. His second objective was to find a facility he could purchase to house scores of other homeless orphans as well as a Christian school.

Upon finding such a place in Nagpur, India, he took a huge leap of faith, borrowing money, hiring a staff, and going through proper legal procedures. He worked with local authorities to identify and gain guardianship of scores of abandoned street children. Then he took almost a hundred of these children and placed them in a facility he named to honor his father. After supervising the opening of the Douglas Memorial Children's Home, he raced back to the United States to raise more funding.

Douglas had no roots and few friends in Dallas. Yet his reputation as an evangelical speaker was well known within Church of God congregations. Using the phone, the balding, bespectacled gentleman begged for a chance to speak to various churches within driving distance of Dallas. He pledged to go out on any day or night. He emphasized that the size of the church did not matter. He just wanted to speak. He had a story to tell, and he trusted that God would provide the venues needed.

By simply sharing his testimony about the Hindu man and the seven orphans, within weeks Douglas had secured enough monthly pledges from churches and individuals to fund his first real children's home. By sending a photograph and case history of each child to the person providing the funding, he also established a link between donor and recipient. He then encouraged donors to write to their sponsored children and had supervisors in India send letters back to those providing support. Through this system, people could see progress, and once-unwanted children felt they had real value.

Though he did not have a grasp of the full potential of what he had begun, Douglas did understand that there was a need for more children's homes. So just as he had in business, he began to expand. But where would he find enough donors to meet his new budget?

Dr. Norman Vincent Peale had established a vast following for his work through fifteen-minute radio programs. Douglas had listened to them on many occasions. He quickly understood why the New York minister's message was so readily accepted. Peale had given his listeners a sense of personal value. He had convinced them that with a little faith, they could rise above their daily problems and do something very special. The problem for many of these new positive thinkers was not a matter of faith—they had it now—it was a matter of works. Where were they going to find something that needed their support?

Douglas's experience in business clearly showed him there was a market for his "product" of compassionate outreach. Now he had to find a way to reach the millions who had the faith but no place to put it to work. That would call for marketing, something else he had learned in the business world. He now began to understand that he had not been ignoring a call, but rather God had given him the experience needed to direct that calling.

Beginning in Dallas, Douglas again took a leap of faith and used his own money to purchase radio time. Employing a mixture of old-fashioned preaching and heartfelt stories of the orphans' plight in India, he found an audience ready to be called to action. As support began to pour in, the evangelist hurried back to India to buy more property and establish more homes. Within just a few years he was taking care of thousands of children in scores of facilities throughout southern India.

Now approaching retirement age, Douglas should have been content to slow down and simply maintain the orphanages he had already constructed. Yet it seemed the call was now expanding. Each time he returned to India, he was confronted by countless men and women asking him why he was trying to save the "throwaways." They didn't understand why an American would care so deeply about Indian children. Douglas's answer was always, "Jesus loves them, and he loves you too."

During his initial crusade in India few had come to know Jesus through his words. Now as Indians watched his homes taking in abandoned children, as they observed these children in school and at play, as they heard their laughter and witnessed their growth, many asked the preacher how they could know this man he called Savior. Sensing it was time to get back behind the pulpit, Douglas led a new series of crusades in India, and this time thousands came forward during his invitation call.

Within five years of Douglas's accepting the first seven orphans, his vision had grown as much as his following had. In the United States and in India, he was finding great support for his orphan care programs. As he built more homes, he saw new opportunities in mission outreach. The American preacher now fully understood that living a sermon was much more powerful than giving one. Thus he began to build clinics for lepers, feed thousands of hungry families from the lowest of the caste system, drill water wells, and support the work of local Christian ministers. As the organization he had founded completed countless projects, again those seeking knowledge about Christ expanded tenfold. Newspapers were now calling Douglas's World Missionary Evangelism the largest evangelical Christian organization in India, but the preacher simply called it "the work." "It's about what God can do," he explained, "not about what I can do."

As he told radio audiences of the amazing successes in India, he was bombarded with speaking requests from thousands of American churches. Once the leader of a small denomination, he now found that his support crossed all denominational lines. Church groups that once had little contact with each other were suddenly joining in a cause to support the work Douglas had started. As that work grew to the point where more than a hundred children's homes had been built and staffed and scores of new churches had been started, Christians from South Korea asked him to come to their nation and begin programs for war orphans. After that came calls from Bangladesh, Mexico, Kenya, and the Philippines.

During one of his initial visits to the Philippines, Douglas had to run through the jungle to escape a band of angry natives intent on killing him. On that same visit he had to fight off jungle diseases, sleep in the open during heavy rainstorms, and scrape by on food pulled from trees or dug from the ground. Yet even though he was in his sixties, nothing stopped him. He now had a calling he was sure of, and wherever there was a need, he was determined to address it. If that meant crawling through jungles, then he was ready to go.

From the moment he was given the seven children until he reached his mid-eighties, there was no time for rest. He kept up his grueling schedule, pushed to expand the work, and delighted in telling the story of God's miracles to anyone who came into his life. On radio and in person, his enthusiasm for living a sermon never waned.

On a spring day in 1988, he spent the day working with his Dallas staff. Though he now had more than two hundred orphanages under his watchful eye, he felt the need to expand even more. He was especially excited about new opportunities in both Latin America and Africa.

Sitting at his desk, he leafed through letters he had recently received from some of those children who had been pulled off the streets thanks to his work. Many were now doctors, lawyers, teachers, preachers, and nurses. Children who had been unwanted and cast out had become leaders in their communities. Some were even giving back to the homes that World Missionary Evangelism had established.

Thinking back more than thirty years, he again saw the face of the Hindu man who had brought those first seven to him. He now wondered if that man had been a messenger from God. Had the man been sent that day to finally give John Douglas the real calling that had been set in motion when he first pulled the bell cord and stoked the fire at a tiny West Virginia church?

Opening his Bible, the aging man pushed his glasses up on his nose and thumbed the well-worn pages. Finding Matthew 25:40–45 he again read the words that had directed a ministry he had begun during a time when he was getting ready to retire.

> And the King shall answer and say unto them, Verily I say unto you, Inasmuch as ye have done it unto one of the least of these my brethren, ye have done it unto me. Then shall he say also unto them on the left hand, Depart from me, ye cursed, into everlasting fire, prepared for the devil and his angels: For I was an hungred, and ye gave me no meat: I was thirsty, and ye gave me no drink: I was a stranger, and ye took me not in: naked, and ye clothed me not: sick, and in prison, and ye visited me not. Then shall they also answer him, saying, Lord, when saw we thee an hungred, or athirst, or a stranger, or naked, or sick, or in prison, and did not minister unto thee? Then shall he answer them, saying, Verily I say unto you, Inasmuch as ye did it not to one of the least of these, ye did it not to me.

Looking up at a young man who had just come into his office, Douglas pointed to the verse and in a soft voice betraying a bit of Southern twang said, "That is what we have tried to do. That's what the work is all about."

In all his years, Douglas had never said "my work"; it had always been "the work." And now the preacher was sure the hand of God had moved him in various directions to prepare him to do this work. Everything in his life had been laid out to bring him to this point.

"A famine is hitting Africa," Douglas explained. "We have to put together a new relief program in this area. And the problem of

AIDS in that region is going to create so many orphaned children. We must get past our prejudice and see this as a mission, an opportunity God has given us, just like the one he gave me through the Hindu man."

Looking around the office, Douglas picked up his hat, put down the Bible, waved at the staff, shook hands with the visitor, and returned to his home. A few hours later, after he had eaten dinner with his family, a strange look came over his face. Clutching his heart, he said, "Not yet, the work ..." A second later he was dead.

Word quickly spread about the preacher's passing. In the United States many friends and associates called and gave their condolences. Thousands sent special gifts in his memory. Yet for Americans the response was more about tribute than grief. After all, the preacher had lived a long and fruitful life. Yet in India the response was much different.

When they heard the news, thousands in Douglas's adopted land fell to the ground weeping. Even those who had never met him in person felt they had lost a family member.

A major southern Indian newspaper ran the story the day after his death with this headline: "John Douglas—Father to a Million Children Dies." Though the number of orphans cared for through his organization was only in the tens of thousands, there were probably more than a million people who came to know the Lord due to the sermons Douglas lived in the third world.

Two decades after his death, World Missionary Evangelism is still supporting the work John E. Douglas began and is heavily involved in what he had longed to do on the day he died. Through the organization he started, African AIDS orphans are being cared for, educated, and given the same kind of devotion Douglas gave those first seven Indian orphans brought to him by a Hindu man intent on challenging the preacher's faith. That challenge was met, a calling was found, and "the work" of faith goes on long after the man of faith completed his earthly journey.

10

JACOB DESHAZER
Forgiving Everything

When he heard the alarm, he knew his mission was about to start. The glorious day had finally come. It was time to bring a lesson to a vile people who had inspired such a deep hatred in his heart that it enflamed Jacob DeShazer's soul. The sun was just rising over the Pacific's choppy waves as DeShazer pulled himself out of his bunk on the USS *Hornet*.

Unlike most who called the aircraft carrier home, he was not a sailor; rather the twenty-nine-year-old Oregon native was a member of the United States Army Air Corps. When he joined the service, he had had no desire to ride the waves; instead he planned on reaching for the stars. Trained as a mechanic and bombardier, he was much more at home in the skies than on the sea, but on this morning of April 18, 1942, the *Hornet*'s deck felt almost as secure as the solid ground of the farm where he was born. His excitement was at fever pitch because he was about to live out a goal. He was going to kill "Japs," and he couldn't wait.

Just a few months before, on December 7, 1941, DeShazer had been peeling potatoes on an army base in Washington. He had just finished taking the skin off a large spud when a radio announcer broke into a morning broadcast to trumpet the mind-numbing news that the Japanese had attacked Pearl Harbor. Hurling the potato against the wall, the private screamed, "They're going to have to pay for this!"

DeShazer had never felt such rage. Over the next few days his hatred grew to the point where he lay awake at night planning payback for this crime. He imagined all kinds of ways to inflict pain on and create mayhem for a people he viewed as demonic and subhuman. He simply couldn't wait for his first mission and his first kill. Yet rather than being shipped out to the Pacific front to let loose the anger consuming his soul, he was sent three thousand miles east.

In Columbia, South Carolina, DeShazer was thrown into advance bombardier training. Except for some time spent drinking with other soldiers, he did his best to live a model life. He figured that the better his behavior, the more likely his chances at getting to take his personal war to the Japanese.

A few weeks after starting training, he was called into the captain's office. Lieutenant Colonel Jimmy Doolittle was assembling a team of twenty men for a secret mission against the Japanese. It would be dangerous and the details were sketchy, but if these volunteers could pull it off, this mission might help the United States win the war.

DeShazer ignored the danger; the only thing he could think about was being able to inflict chaos. Did he want to do it? Of course he did. When volunteers were asked to step forward, he didn't hesitate. He couldn't wait to draw Japanese blood.

The several months of training in Florida stoked his hatred. Finally, with the smells of spring in the air, DeShazer returned to the West Coast, where he was told he and his fellow volunteers would be manning sixteen B-25s that would be launched from an aircraft carrier in America's first attempt to inflict damage on the Japanese homeland. His job would be to drop bombs on the very people he had come to loathe.

On April 1, 1942, Doolittle and his men watched their planes being loaded on the USS *Hornet*. As anticipation pushed their adrenaline, few considered the odds against them. Yet as the days passed, DeShazer and the others began to fully grasp what they were risking.

A B-25 had never taken off from an aircraft carrier. Because the Americans wanted to hit the Japanese quickly and with surprising force, there had been no time to see if this type of takeoff could even be accomplished. As the pilots studied the carrier's short deck, many of them were now worried the planes would end up in the sea, not in the air. Worse yet, there was no way a B-25 could land on the *Hornet*. So once in the air, the planes would have to find a different place to come down. Yet the fears that these two problems raised paled in comparison to what DeShazer felt when he was given the complete plans.

The length of the trip to the Japanese mainland, even from a point four hundred miles off the island nation, meant there was no turning back. This was a one-way trip. The crews would drop their bombs and then have to fly deep enough into China to get beyond the parts of that country occupied by the Japanese. If they ran out of gas before making the Chinese airfields, the men would drop right into enemy hands. DeShazer now knew that this might be a suicide mission. Still, he wanted to go. If he died, at least he would perish while dealing a huge blow to the nation that had attacked America.

Because everything about the raid was cloaked in secrecy, none of the volunteers could inform their families of what they were attempting. They had to bear the weight of the odds with no outside help. There were no goodbyes, no final "I love you's," no chance to write that last letter explaining the situation to wives, mothers, or sweethearts. They were as alone as any group could be. In the moments before the launch, their only real companions were thoughts of their own mortality.

The winds were strong and the seas rough as dawn broke that April day, and the *Hornet* was still two hundred miles from the mission's proposed launch point. Admiral Bull Halsey was concerned. He had already sent a ship out to sink two enemy destroyers. Now a lookout had spotted another Japanese vessel. After the losses they had suffered at Pearl Harbor, the navy could not afford to lose the *Hornet*.

With that in mind, the admiral summoned the unflappable Doolittle. As the two men spoke, Halsey informed him that the carrier could go no farther. The risk was too great. Doolittle could postpone the raid and turn back or launch it knowing his planes had so much more distance to cover that few of them would likely make it out of Japanese territory before having to ditch. A placid Doolittle smiled, shook Halsey's hand, and gave the order to start the mission.

A few minutes later the *Hornet* turned into the wind, and Doolittle piloted the first bomber off the deck. Most were shocked when the plane stayed in the air. Fourteen more followed before DeShazer and his crew got their chance to join the battle.

DeShazer's plane, number 16, had been tied at the far back of the deck with its tail hanging off the ship and over the sea. When the crew got it ready for takeoff, the plane, christened *The Bat out of Hell*, almost fell into the Pacific. It took scores of navy personnel pulling on ropes to keep it on the deck, and none of them noticed when a gaping hole was punched into its nose when it hit the deck. It might have been airworthy, but it was certainly not aerodynamic. The problem should have been obvious, but in the haste to get the bird into the air, no one made a final inspection of the last B-25.

When number 16's crew launched, they finally noticed the problem. But by then it was too late; they couldn't land on the *Hornet*. The damage cost them speed and precious fuel while putting their lives at even greater risk. Still, they pushed toward the city of Nagoya.

At just past one o'clock, the slowed bomber finally arrived at the target. Maybe the problem with the nose meant they wouldn't survive this mission, but at least DeShazer would feel the rush of pulling the lever and dropping his bombs on the unsuspecting people below. He checked his equipment, his heart pumping so fast that he felt it might explode. As the targets came into view, he realized that this wonderful moment was what he had dreamed of since Pearl Harbor. His time for revenge and retribution had finally arrived. And he would be the one to release the bombs.

The first incendiary bomb hit an oil refinery. As DeShazer watched it burn, a great sense of satisfaction filled him. The remainder of his load was dropped on a factory. Smoke filled the skies, and the wounded plane and its exhilarated crew turned toward China.

Now the men were living on borrowed time. In just a matter of hours they would run out of fuel. After the last of the precious liquid was finally sucked into the engines, the crew of *The Bat out of Hell* would either die or find themselves in the hands of an angry enemy.

The sun had set by the time the final engine began to die. No one wanted to toss themselves out of the plane and parachute into the darkness not knowing what was below. Yet with the plane now sputtering, there was no choice. One by one they floated away from the B-25 into a hell on earth that they couldn't have imagined in their darkest nightmares. This crew quickly discovered that triumph and tragedy are separated by a thin line.

As he drifted to the ground, DeShazer was blown away from the rest of his crew. He landed in darkness so black, he didn't even see the ground rush up to meet him. As he landed, he fractured his ribs. Struggling to his feet, he realized that he didn't know the difference between a Japanese person and a Chinese person. He also had no understanding of either country's customs. How would he be able to tell whether the first person he met was friend or foe?

Shooting his gun into the air, he waited for a reply from one of his team. The silence was deafening; he was alone. Others might have prayed when facing this kind of situation, but God was little more than an abstract thought in DeShazer's mind; his faith was in his gun and in the members of his crew. Where were they? Confused, the downed flyer wandered into a village, where he was met by smiling Asian soldiers. For the moment he felt safe and lowered his gun. Only after these new friends pointed their rifles at him did he realize his mistake.

The Japanese army now had the man who had dropped bombs on one of its cities. After being interrogated for hours, DeShazer was ushered to a place where he met the other members of his crew. The reunion was short-lived. The next day they were flown to Japan for a show trial and housed individually in isolated cells.

Legal authorities in Japan debated for days in trying to decide if the Americans were prisoners of war or common criminals. For DeShazer and his comrades, the argument seemed absurd. In their minds, the distinction was not worth considering. But the Japanese military had its reasons for wanting the men treated as if they had been caught after a crime. If they were considered civilians, then the prosecution could use far more severe methods of interrogation than if the bomber crew was viewed as military personnel caught on a mission.

Ultimately the courts ruled they were soldiers and had to be treated as such. Thus Doolittle's Raiders legally had more rights, but as they soon found out, few of those rights were recognized or granted. As the sham proceedings concluded, the judge happily informed DeShazer that he was guilty of all crimes, that he was to die by beheading, and that the judge, even though he was a kind and gentle man, was to personally handle his execution.

The American airman calmly replied, "It would be the greatest honor to have the kindest judge in Japan cut off my head." Japanese officers laughed as the judge signaled for DeShazer to be removed.

Taken to an isolation cell, DeShazer was blindfolded and handcuffed. A few hours later, at a time when he expected to meet death by the sword, he and his fellow crewmembers were led to a plane and flown back to Japanese occupied China.

For several months DeShazer and his crew languished in Shanghai, living in horrid conditions, given little to eat, and beaten for sport. They were little more than skin and bones by the time they were returned to Nagasaki for another round of Japanese justice. At the end of the second trial, the men were again given the death sentence. They no doubt would have been shot by a firing squad if the emperor had not quickly reduced a majority of the sentences, including DeShazer's, to life. Yet the three men deemed most important to the mission did not feel the favor of the Japanese ruler and were executed.

DeShazer was in solitary confinement, picking lice off his body and eating only a bowl of rice a day, when he was given the news he was not to be killed. But his joy was tempered by a wave of hopelessness. Yes, he would live, but that meant more abuse, suffering, and loneliness. At times he wondered if a quick death would be better than starvation, disease, or torture.

With no explanation, the Americans were taken back to the Japanese POW prison. It was October 1942, and for DeShazer the war was really just beginning. Alone with his thoughts, he harbored a hatred for the Japanese, which fueled a desire to survive so great that it allowed him to fight through illness, hunger, and depression. His hate simply would not let him die.

As he sat in his dark cell, hunger eating away at his bones, rats scampering just a few inches from his feet, DeShazer often thought back to his youth in Oregon. He was born on November 15, 1912. His father had been a Church of God minister and full-time farmer in Salem. Maybe if his dad had lived longer, Jacob would have known a bit more about the faith that drove the man. But the older DeShazer died when Jacob was only three. Two years later his mother remarried, and they moved to a windswept community on the Oregon prairie. With a population of barely over a hundred souls, Madras offered the boy few outlets but school and church. At the time he cared little for either.

As he grew into his teens, cigarettes and alcohol offered a way for him to rebel, but DeShazer was hardly wild. Only after graduation, when he worked a series of jobs across the West Coast, did he begin to enjoy the nightlife and good times with rough friends at bars. Yet like the dead-end jobs he worked during the Depression, even his nights drinking with buddies offered little satisfaction. So in 1939, after failing as a farmer, the young man said goodbye to his family and friends and enlisted in the army. That was how he had ended up at McChord Field on December 7, 1941.

Until the attack on Pearl Harbor, DeShazer's experience in the military contained little direction and almost no passion. He was simply drifting along, satisfied to use his paychecks for cigarettes, beer, and card games. He had no dreams and no real ambition. Then the attack brought out a hate stronger than any emotion DeShazer had ever known. And now, just months later in a small prison cell, as he rubbed ribs that were sore from being kicked and as he picked at scores of scabs caused by malnutrition, that hate was growing stronger. For the moment the focal point had been narrowed from all things Japanese to the guard who paced just outside his door.

In the darkness, DeShazer spent hours each day conceiving new ways to kill the man who brought him his maggot-filled bowl of rice. He tried to invent methods for murder that would prolong pain and suffering for hours, if not days. Over time he expanded his murderous desires to include every one of the camp workers, then all those who were occupying China, and finally every man, woman, and child in Japan. DeShazer now believed that the only way he would ever really be happy was to have the planet stripped of every living member of the Japanese race.

Occasionally DeShazer was allowed to mix with the other men from the Doolittle plane crews. One of those men, Lieutenant Bob Meder, confused DeShazer. Meder was polite and respectful to those who abused him. He thanked them for the meager portions of spoiled rice and the ragged clothes. He asked them about their families. He smiled at them when they cursed him, and he did not show any anger when they beat him. In DeShazer's mind, the once almost-heroic Meder now seemed weak. How had this man, the same one who reportedly had been so courageous when saving the lives of his own crew during a crash landing after the raid, now been transformed into a pawn? Why didn't he cling to the same hate that drove DeShazer and the others?

During the fourteen months after their mock trial, Meder grew weaker and weaker in body, but he maintained his friendly resolve. Whenever the men were given a chance to visit, DeShazer tried to comfort his friend by dreaming aloud of the day they would get the opportunity to beat and torture their guards. What a great day that would be!

Meder always shook his head at this idea. In a feeble voice he would say, "They don't know about Jesus. They don't know about his love. They haven't read the Bible. Don't hate them; you need to pray for them and to show Christ in your actions toward them."

Meder's words made little impact on DeShazer until the lieutenant finally died of malnutrition and disease. DeShazer was shocked when the guards seemed genuinely upset by Meder's passing. The Japanese soldiers built a coffin to hold his body and placed a spray of flowers and a Bible on the wooden box. And when they brought the remaining four members of the bombing crews into the dead man's cell, the guards even asked if certain prayers might be said in the man's honor.

As he stared at the coffin, DeShazer began to wonder about what Meder had said. DeShazer had gone to Sunday school as a child. He knew a few Bible verses, but that knowledge had not changed his life. This man had seemingly taken his knowledge of God to heart. It had brought him comfort and peace. How had words on a page done this?

"It was soon after Meder's death," DeShazer later wrote, "that I began to ponder the cause of such hatred between members of the human race. I wondered what it was that made the Japanese hate the Americans and what made me hate the Japanese. My thoughts turned toward what I had heard about Christianity changing hatred between human beings into real brotherly love, and I was gripped with a strange longing to examine the Christian's Bible to see if I could find the secret."

Seized by an illogical and unfathomable passion stronger even than his hate for the Japanese, DeShazer began to ask his captors if he could read the Bible placed on Meder's coffin. For months he begged to get a look at the book, pleading time and time again for just the opportunity to study those words if only for a few days. In time that thirst for the knowledge and hope Meder had found in the Bible became deeper than DeShazer's need for food or his desire for freedom. Reading the book was almost all he thought about. Nothing else now mattered.

Alone, trapped in a cell smaller than some beds, he studied the bit of light coming through a tiny opening near the top of the ceiling. As he did, he desperately thought back to those long-ago Sunday school classes. What were those verses in those lessons? As his mind drew blanks, he began to mentally beat himself up for not being a better student. If he had just paid attention, if he had just treated those moments in that tiny church with the importance they deserved, then he would know those verses now. If he knew them, he just might have the answers Meder seemed to have.

Fall turned to winter and the cell grew cold. Sleeping on a damp floor with no heat, DeShazer became so sick that he was sure he would die. It had been hate that drove him to survive the previous winters; now what sustained him day after miserable day was the need to know the secrets hidden in the Bible.

With spring came not only stifling heat that turned his quarters into an oven but also scores of painful boils. Death cried out to him, beckoning him to race toward the end by taking his own life. Yet even on the days when his fever made him almost delirious and weakness prevented him from standing, DeShazer still begged his guards for access to the Bible. Before he died, he had to know what was in that book.

Finally, in May 1944, the prisoner was given the well-worn Bible in which Meder had found such peace. He was told he could have it for just three weeks; then he would have to return it to the guard.

The fact that his cell had little light didn't deter DeShazer. He found a way to shimmy up the wall to the light at the top of his ceiling. There, with his legs and back pushing opposite walls, he read for hours. In less than a week he made it from the first words in Genesis to the last words in Revelation. He read many of the books over and over again, trying to memorize each verse while attempting to glean what there was in these passages that had so driven Meder's attitude and life.

Then on June 8, 1944, DeShazer was struck by a truth he had never before understood. God loved him and was with him even in this Japanese prison. Turning to Romans 10:9, he read these words out loud: "If thou shalt confess with thy mouth the Lord Jesus, and shalt believe in thine heart that God hath raised him from the dead, thou shalt be saved."

Hungry, dirty, covered with sores, trapped behind bars, and living in filth, DeShazer suddenly felt as if he could fly. His heart soared as he cried with joy. He later described what he experienced on this special day.

"In that very moment God gave me grace to confess my sins to him, and he forgave me all my sins and saved me for Jesus' sake, even as I later found that his Word again promises so clearly in 1 John 1:9: 'If we confess our sins, he is faithful and just to forgive us our sins, and to cleanse us from all unrighteousness.'

"How my heart rejoiced in my newness of spiritual life, even though my body was suffering so terribly from the physical beatings and lack of food. But suddenly I discovered that God had given me new spiritual eyes, and that when I looked at the Japanese officers and guards who had starved and beaten me and my companions so cruelly, I found my bitter hatred for them changed to loving pity. I realized that these Japanese did not know anything about my Savior and that if Christ is not in a heart, it is natural to be cruel. I read in my Bible that while those who crucified Jesus on the cross had beaten him and spit upon him before he was nailed to the cross, he tenderly prayed in his moment of excruciating suffering, 'Father, forgive them, for they know not what they do.' And now from the depths of my heart, I too prayed for God to forgive my torturers."

A few days later it rained. Climbing back to his small window to watch a violent thunderstorm, DeShazer allowed the wet, cool drops to blow onto his face. As the water rolled down his brow and onto his shoulders, he again confessed his sins. He was sure that God had sent the rain to baptize him and symbolically wash away all those past sins, especially his hatred of the Japanese. Now he knew the peace that he had seen in Meder. Now he understood the joy and power of faith.

Yet in war, peace rarely lasts for more than a few moments. An angry guard used DeShazer as a punching bag. This time, rather than fight back, the American remembered the words of 1 Corinthians 13 and took the beating without complaint. Keeping God's love in his mind and heart, the next time he saw the guard, he smiled and inquired as to the man's health. Over the next few weeks DeShazer asked the guard about his family, and as much as possible, the two formed a bond. Soon this relationship bridged a gap between the two enemies as the guard began to give the prisoner extra rations. He even brought in a doctor to help treat the American's sores. DeShazer's transformation had been initiated by watching the way Meder acted, and now the guard was responding to this attitude as well.

Not long after his conversion, the remaining captive members of Doolittle's Raiders were moved north to a better, cleaner facility.

On August 10, as DeShazer prayed in his cell for peace, he was overcome with a feeling of joy. Suddenly strength welled up in his weakened body. He even heard a voice saying, "You don't have to worry, the war is won." Ten days later Americans came into his camp and freed the four remaining flyers. His ordeal was over. He would never have to set foot on Japanese soil again. He could go home.

Unlike so many others who had been held in the wretched conditions of prison camps, DeShazer did not want to turn on those who had judged and abused him. Instead he felt a need to reach out to them. While others slugged or spat on their guards, he shook their hands and even embraced them.

DeShazer was now sure that if the Japanese just knew about Jesus, their lives and actions would dramatically change. But how could he possibly start a mission to reach a people who had brought so much death and destruction to the United States? Yet, strangely, he now felt that was what he had been called to do. He believed that was why his plane had been damaged and he had not had the fuel to fly to safety. It was why Meder had been in that prison. All along, God had been showing DeShazer a direction for his life.

Like many, DeShazer at first found excuses for not listening to the call. Yet the voice he heard in his heart would not let him alone. The saving message he had seen lived out by Lieutenant Meder was something he knew had to be lived again in his life. He had been a prisoner of the Japanese for more than three years, and he was only alive because the emperor had spared him from a death sentence. So who better to show the miracle of God's love and the transforming power of faith to the Japanese than Jacob DeShazer?

He told the details of his salvation experience to reporters who gathered to interview the heroic former POWs who had flown with Doolittle. Because of this press coverage, he was asked to share the story in churches. When he informed those groups he wanted to go into missionary work, Seattle Pacific College offered him a scholarship. Everything seemed to fall into place.

As a student, he met a young woman who also wanted to do missionary work. They were married and began to explore options for Christian service. As DeShazer gained confidence in his talents, he wrote a short story called "I Was a Prisoner of Japan" that included the details of his conversion and his desire to go back to Japan and share Jesus with a people he had once hated. This story led to his being given support for that mission.

In 1948 DeShazer returned to the island nation he had once bombed. Along with his wife and newborn son, he was ready to reach out to a people he had once vowed to kill. He figured that finding just one person to listen to his story might take years, so he was shocked when thousands of Japanese men and women were waiting at the docks to meet him.

DeShazer's "I Was a Prisoner of Japan" had been reprinted as a Christian tract. More than a million copies of his testimony had already been distributed to the Japanese people. Two of those greeting him upon his return to their country were former prison guards who had once beaten DeShazer. Thanks to his kindness after his conversion and the tract he had written, they had been saved. Thousands of others followed.

In the second year of DeShazer's work in Japan, Mitsuo Fuchida was saved. Fuchida was the Japanese naval flier who had led the raid on Pearl Harbor, and he too read "I Was a Prisoner of Japan." As the two met and hugged, the war finally seemed to end.

DeShazer raised his family in Japan and continued his work of evangelism. He gave the energy of his life to the same nation that had once treated him worse than an unwanted dog. While his initial bombing run had almost no impact on the events of World War II, his second mission made an impression that is still being felt to this day.

Jacob DeShazer was ninety-five when he died on March 15, 2008, at his home in Salem, Oregon. His passing was noted all across Japan as the people there both honored his memory and celebrated the legacy started when an everlasting light was found in a dark prison cell. For many Christians in Japan, the roots of their faith can be traced to the bombardier of a B-25 called *The Bat out of Hell*.

11

ROBERT RAIKES
Teaching Millions

R obert Raikes was the forty-four-year-old publisher of the *Gloucester Journal* when he took a Sunday ride into the country looking for a man he could hire as a gardener. The sun was bright, the air heavy, and just a hint of breeze stirred up the dust of the road on that typical English morning in 1781.

The outgoing Raikes was well known in his community, not only for his strong, often biting editorial campaigns but also for his wealth. The publisher had become rich the old-fashioned way: he had inherited a fortune from his father. Yet rather than sink in a world of debauchery, using his inheritance as a means of living the high life, this husband and father had employed his resources to serve the underprivileged in the area.

Nowhere had his concern and compassion been more evident than when he led a fight for the rights of prisoners at the local jail. That editorial-driven battle had initially caused a drop in his paper's circulation because his crusade proved to be unpopular, especially with his wealthy peers. But Raikes didn't care about the financial toll; he was simply interested in seeking Christian justice.

Raikes's push for prison reform was not based on church-learned morality. He saw the movement as logical. He argued that prisoners were resources who, if properly trained, could find a place in and serve society. With skills given them during their incarceration, they could eventually secure honest work. Investing in men while they were behind bars would benefit everyone by creating a more peaceful community. This made more sense than starving and beating prisoners, thus creating men who were even more violent and releasing them on the streets. No one was safe if this continued.

Surprisingly, Raikes's campaign was so successful that Gloucester went so far as to create educational programs in the city prison facilities. This was something the publisher was proud to hang his hat on. But that was yesterday's news; now he had to find a gardener to keep his estate from becoming an overgrown eyesore.

As he knocked on the door of the modest rural home, Raikes surveyed the well-kept grounds. Just then a tiny woman answered the door.

"You must be Mr. Raikes," she said.

"Yes."

"My husband had to leave for a few minutes, but he will be back soon. Would you like to come in and wait?"

The publisher shook his head. "No, thank you. I think I'll just sit out here and enjoy the view of your gardens."

The quietness of the pastoral scene, the beauty and clean smells of nature, filled the man's senses. In the city where he worked, noise was a constant. This was a moment he wanted to treasure.

But the tranquility was temporary, soon replaced by the screams of children out for a Sunday romp. As they rounded the bend and came into view, Raikes was shocked. The dozen or so boys, ranging in age from six to twelve, were dirty, unkempt, and angry. Cursing like hardened sailors, they pushed and shoved each other, viciously picking on the weakest members of the ragtag army. When a small child was knocked off his feet, those left standing laughed and made fun of him, kicking dirt into his face.

Raikes had seen this same kind of behavior during his trips to the local prison. Yet in those cases it had been men involved in destructive actions; now it was mere lads.

Looking back at the woman, he asked, "Who are these boys?"

"They're vermin," she told him. "They work in the factories during the week and then raise holy hell on Sunday. You can't even go to church without hearing their vulgar voices. They break windows, steal us blind, and taunt us when we try to stop them. They need to be rounded up and put away."

"What about their families?"

"Those demons pretty much raise themselves. Their folks don't care. They're no better than street trash themselves. And they are taking over too. We are being overrun by this kind of trash."

A few hours later, as Raikes returned to his home, he took a detour through the main part of Gloucester. Thanks to the Industrial Revolution, the city had doubled in population over the past twenty years. The publisher had initially chalked up the growth as a wonderful bonus for the city and its business. But now as he observed hundreds of filthy urchins mindlessly wandering the streets, he saw the other side of the growth.

These children, who were working in the factories twelve hours a day, six days a week, were treated like animals by their employers. They also had no chance at an education, had never been taught any manners, and evidently had no guidance at home. They were mean, surly, disrespectful, and amoral. Worse yet, more were coming to town each week. So the problem was going to multiply. Something had to be done.

Days later, sitting down with local business and community leaders, Raikes asked about the street kids. The responses he received were often laced with profanity. Sunday, once the best day of the week, was now dreaded. These children were heathen, little better than rats. The rage caused by them, even among the clergy, was sobering.

Raikes realized the children were not going anywhere. The factory bosses had to have them to manufacture their goods. So if the answer was not in forced removal and relocation, what was it? What could make the dramatic change needed to save this new generation of children that had been created by the Industrial Age?

A month later, while sitting at his desk pondering what he now saw and heard on the streets each Sunday, the publisher attempted to compose an editorial addressing the issue. Yet the only word he scratched out with his pen on a piece of paper was *try*. One word did not an editorial make, and so the paper ended up in the trash. Even to a man as brilliant as Raikes, there seemed to be no answer other than hiring more law enforcement officers on Sunday. Yet there had to be a better way. As it stood, most of these children were destined for the very prison he had helped clean up. Ironically, only behind bars would they have a chance to gain the tools they needed to become productive citizens.

Over the next few weeks the word *try* kept echoing in the publisher's mind. It haunted him as he wrote, as he ate meals, and even as he attended church. Ultimately he became convinced that an inner voice was ordering him to try to save the children. This was to be his new cause, but where could he start? Even as a publisher, with all the power of the press, he seemed helpless. So for weeks while his desire to help increased, his hope of finding a way to inspire a positive change diminished.

One day he stopped by the local jail to check on the reforms enacted there. As he watched the well-behaved convicts, he realized that keeping the street kids busy, giving them something productive to do, and offering them a chance to improve themselves was the key to bringing peace back to Sundays. After all, if it was working with convicted criminals, why not with rowdy children?

When he returned home, Raikes looked at his own ten children. They were polite, respectful, and bright. That was because they had been raised in a clean, moral environment where they had been loved and educated. They had values because they had been taught them. If he could somehow teach these street kids some values, then they might be changed as well. At the very least it was an experiment worth attempting on a small scale.

In a section of the city known as Sooty Alley due to its decay and filth, Raikes gathered a few dozen children, hired a local schoolteacher, and found an empty building for a classroom. Underwriting the cost of the school himself, he got the children to attend by promising a noon meal, new clothing, and the chance to learn to read. The only requirement for the students was that they be respectful during their time at the school. Since the only available time for the learning sessions was Sunday, Raikes had his teacher use the Bible as the curriculum.

As the weeks went by and the people who lived and walked in the areas around Sooty Alley noted that the streets were again quiet, they began to wonder what happened to the children who had once plagued them at every corner. When they discovered that Raikes had them in school, a few were happy, but surprisingly, many more were appalled.

Businesses were not allowed to open on Sunday. This was the law. The law had been influenced by the church, which wanted to make sure people could attend Sunday services. Because Raikes was paying the teacher, she was breaking both city and church laws by working on Sunday. So even though his Sunday school sessions were making a huge dent in local crime, a large portion of the community, including several churches, wanted the facility shut down and a specific law passed that forbade the opening of any more such schools.

Raikes had been a solid, well-read student before entering the publishing field. The only reason he did not finish his studies at Cambridge was his father's death. Not only was he a good writer, but he knew the Bible better than anyone, even the clergy. So as he waged his new war of ideas, the publisher pulled out a number of examples of Sabbath schools dating back to even before the start of the organized church. He showed how even Jesus attended one of these schools on the Sabbath.

Raikes also showed how some churches used Sunday services to instruct children in biblical principles. Because his school used the Bible as its textbook, he too was teaching children about Christianity. He argued that Christian education was the one hope these children had to escape a life of crime. His idea was also the only way he saw to reclaim the peaceful Sundays that had once been such a treasured part of life in Gloucester. Finally, when the criticism continued but no one offered a better alternative, he asked for time to prove that his concept would create lasting and meaningful change. A majority of those in the city agreed to give him a few months to prove his program had merit.

With the success he had already seen, Raikes wanted to expand beyond the Sooty area. He realized he needed two things to take his program citywide. The first was money, which he had. The second was a plan. He had created the first school on the fly, with little real thought to doing anything more than seeing if children would sit still from ten o'clock on Sunday morning until five in the afternoon. With the small, handpicked group it was working. But before he took it to hundreds, he needed to put together a plan that included goals and ways to reach them.

The publisher's first and primary goal was to create good citizens of the street children. Raikes knew that almost all of the kids were beaten and abused at home and on the job. So his first rule for his Sunday schools was that teachers were to use only positive reinforcement, with rewards employed to change behavior. Those rewards would be items the children would treasure, like new shoes, clothes, combs, and candy. The students would earn these rewards by being respectful to their teacher and classmates, by not using profanity, and by doing well in their lessons.

Each teacher should gently push children to see their studies as a duty, thus improving their ambition so they could envision a life beyond the shabby lot that had been theirs since birth. Raikes also asked his teachers to find ways to encourage civic responsibility. He knew that if he could achieve the latter, he could eventually gain community and church support for his project. The change of a hoodlum into a model citizen would prove the value of his idea. Thus he saw God's Word as the best printed model for this endeavor.

For Raikes, using the Bible as the primary source of educating his charges had little to do with trying to spread faith. In truth the publisher considered himself a "thoughtful believer." Faith played little or no part in why he called himself a Christian. Instead Raikes liked the morality and the order he saw in following Christ's lead. Good behavior brought peace to a family and community. Following God's laws created the proper environment for business. Giving to the poor paved the way for respect and lowered crime rates. For Raikes, Christianity was the most logical process to achieve a society that functioned for the good of everyone. Yet faith, which was supposed to be such an important facet of Christianity, was something the man rarely mentioned or even considered. He thought of himself as a man of ideas and action. To him, faith was far too abstract a concept to play an important role in his daily life.

Within a year, thanks to his money and enthusiasm, Raikes watched his initial Sunday school spawn three more. Sixty students had now blossomed into several hundred. In much of the city, the streets were again peaceful on Sunday, and the discussion of the Sunday schools as being unlawful or immoral ended.

This success prompted Raikes to publish an editorial on the new program in the *Gloucester Journal* in 1783. The front-page piece did what it was intended to do: the Sunday school movement quickly gathered support from nobility, the area's businessmen, and even the factory owners. As the newspaper article was reprinted by other newspapers and periodicals across England, other communities jumped on board. Within a year there were eighteen hundred students in schools in Manchester and Salford. Twelve months later there were thousands more in similar programs from Scotland to Wales. Most were using Raikes's concepts in their teaching, and some were even obtaining the materials and books he was publishing for his schools in Gloucester.

It was the books Raikes created that really gave wings to his movement. His primers, spelling books, readers, youth Bibles, and materials on catechism gave schools a uniform way to reach the goals the publisher saw as important. Through the use of Christianity, children could be taught to be good citizens. As crime rates dropped in every community where Sunday schools were established, Raikes's ideas proved their merit.

A few years into his grand experiment, Raikes found his mailbox overflowing with hundreds of letters from men and women wanting to know how to start Sunday schools in their own communities. Still, even though the changes many pastors saw were dramatic, churches shied away from getting involved. To many Christian leaders of the day, these Sunday schools still seemed to have a secular feel to them, even though the Bible was being used as a teaching guide. Many even felt they were demonic in nature.

This view dramatically changed when pastors took a deeper look at the children who had graduated from these programs. As young adults, the former students were not just good citizens; they were practicing their faith. They were attending church, raising their own families to revere the Bible, and embracing Jesus as their Savior. It wasn't just their minds that had been changed by Raikes's logical education; their hearts had been changed too.

Witnessing that kind of transformation inspired scores of churches to open their doors to the Sunday school program. In just one generation after the beginning of the Sooty school, denominations were publishing Sunday school materials for their own churches, and hundreds of thousands of children were enrolled in the classes. In what was then seen as a revolutionary idea, churches even began to seek out the children of poor, heathen families, transporting them to Sunday school and taking an active interest in their lives. Churches that in the past had all but ignored the poorest of the poor were now seeking them out. Sunday schools had created a revolution in the way congregations reached out in the community.

Raikes was naturally pleased with the results of his great experiment. As Sunday schools were exported from Britain to Europe and

America, he began to understand the power of this vision spurred on by the word *try*. This was probably his greatest accomplishment. Yet the joy he gained from this success was rooted in his mind, not his heart. His goal had always been to use Christianity to mold citizens, not to empower children with the knowledge of a living God. The latter was not a concept the publisher understood. Yet the same schools that revolutionized childhood outreach and presented faith to hundreds of millions also opened the door for Raikes's own spiritual growth.

Long after he had established his movement, the publisher still made a habit of visiting his schools unannounced to view the work firsthand. One Sunday as Raikes quietly observed scores of children eagerly doing their lessons, he noted a small girl in a far corner whispering as she read from a book. With her piercing blue eyes focused on the words, the poorly dressed child didn't notice the newspaper editor approach.

Leaning close to hear what she was reading, Raikes immediately recognized the words. It was Isaiah 53. As he heard her slowly work her way through the passage, it was as if he were hearing these words for the very first time. Looking into the girl's face, he sensed that she wasn't just reading them; she was feeling them. They were impacting her in a way that went beyond logic. For this child, Sunday school was not just a rational place of peace; it was a spiritual home.

Suddenly there was a presence around him, a warmth he had never known and a joy he had never felt. His heart began to race, his mouth grew parched, and his blood rushed through his body. God was alive! He now knew it. For the first time, this feeling wasn't just in his head; it was in his heart as well. It was God who had told him to try. It was God who had showed him the way.

For the first time in his life, Raikes was overcome with emotion created by faith. As he fell to his knees beside the little girl, he realized that his schools had not just brought civility to thousands of children; the schools had brought a living Christ into their lives. That was why the children had changed. And now a child who had found Jesus in one of his schools was introducing Raikes himself to the power of faith.

With faith now stoking his logic, Raikes immersed himself in making sure the spiritual nature of his schools was emphasized above every other facet of the curriculum. He now clearly saw what he had created in following Jesus' instructions to "feed my lambs."

In 1788, just seven years after the Sooty school began and with the movement already spreading across the globe, John Wesley said of Raikes's greatest legacy, "I verily think these Sunday schools are one of the noblest specimens of charity which have been set on foot in England since William the Conqueror."

A generation later Raikes looked at what he had initiated and said, "The world marches forth on the feet of little children, but who can doubt that there is today a desperately important educational task for the children, whether through the Sunday school, or some other format. To change the world—reach the children!

"If the glory of God be promoted in any, even the smallest degree, society must reap some benefit. If the good seed be sown in the mind at an early period of human life though it shows itself not again for many years, it may please God, at some future period, to cause it to spring up, and to bring forth a plentiful harvest."

By Raikes's death in 1811, just thirty years after he drew up plans for his first school, more than half a million children were regularly attending Sunday school in Great Britain. Twenty years later that number had grown to a point where a quarter of the English population attended Sunday school once a week.

As a teaching and soul-saving dynamic of the modern church, nothing comes close to having the impact of Sunday schools. For more than two centuries they have been the most powerful tool in educating children about every facet of Christianity. Countless millions who otherwise never would have heard the Word found Christ through the efforts of a Sunday school teacher. These classes have become the primary birthplace of teachers, preachers, and missionaries. Yet Raikes has impacted every child in the free world in another way that he had not foreseen.

First in England and then in the United States, Raikes's Sunday school model and the results it produced created a movement for free public education. Children who once went to work before their teens were taken out of factories and fields and placed into schools. The educational system we have today was spun off of Raikes's Sunday schools.

A trip to interview a gardener opened up the door to faith as no other movement ever has. The legacy of this small-town publisher is still being realized every time a Sunday school teacher presents a new lesson in faith to one of his or her pupils. What Raikes gave a few ragged kids in Gloucester paved the way for salvation for hundreds of millions, including his own. Few have left the world with a greater legacy of faith than Robert Raikes.

12

FRED ROGERS
Providing a Home

Francis of Assisi is reputed to have said, "Preach the gospel at all times; if necessary, use words." This direct, simple assessment of faith, spoken nine centuries before the advent of television, would come to fit Fred Rogers as comfortably as any sweater he owned. The ordained preacher, whose very basic sermons were presented five times a week on national television, was born in Latrobe, Pennsylvania. This gentle man became the video version of the Good Samaritan and in the process changed the lives of millions of children. But before he became a national icon, Rogers had to survive childhood.

As a youngster, Rogers was shy and fat. Born in 1928 and growing up in the Depression, his social and physical disabilities made him an easy target for the verbal and physical assaults of classmates. In 1936, while running fearfully through the streets with a pack of boys yelling threats behind him, Rogers felt sure that this time the charging bullies would not just bring him to his knees but knock him on his back. Freddy, as he was then known, raced along sidewalks and down alleys, barely keeping ahead of the bullies. His breath coming hard, his strength giving out, he made his way to a row of familiar houses. He knew most of the families who lived in this neighborhood and even went to church with some of them. In fact, just ahead lived a kind woman who talked to him on a regular basis. If he could just make it to her porch . . .

On that spring day, when that grandmotherly figure answered his knock, Freddy was spared the wrath of an unfriendly and hostile world. That lesson of refuge and safety found in the safe haven of a familiar neighborhood one day blossomed into an idea for reaching small children through an exciting new medium. Yet before that could transpire, Freddy had to absorb several other critical life lessons.

Freddy, the only son of James and Nancy Rogers, was close to his parents, who were outstanding mentors and Christian role models. But he also spent a great deal of his spare time with his grandfather, Fred McFeely. Fred taught his grandson how to make and bring to life the puppets he one day wove into his famed television program. His grandfather also taught him a great deal about the importance of respecting all forms of life.

From his mother Freddy learned an appreciation for music. When he was nine, Nancy enrolled her son in piano lessons. Soon the boy was not only playing the melodies assigned for his practice sessions but also composing simple tunes. In fact, the piano provided much of the therapy that helped Rogers through the difficult days of being bullied by schoolmates. Whenever his anger or embarrassment built up to the boiling point, he rushed to the keyboard and took out his frustrations on the ivories.

His mother and father also took Freddy to church each week. In Sunday school and worship services, Freddy observed how much prayer and Bible study meant to his family. He also came to see that the lessons he was taught at church were played out in the way his parents lived each day of their lives. Never was this more evident than when they added a very special new member to their family.

In the midst of the Great Depression a young boy's mother passed away, leaving him orphaned. James and Nancy knew the family and stepped up to adopt the child rather than see him placed in a children's home. With little fanfare George became an older brother to the shy and bullied Freddy. As such, he became his protector and his role model. The fact that George was an African-American growing up with a white family opened Fred's mind to the fact that God knows no color or race—we all are his children. It seemed that from that instant Rogers felt a brotherhood with all men.

This lesson of compassion was probably the greatest and most lasting one his parents ever gave Rogers. It brought into focus the other events of his life and pushed him in a direction to live out his faith by reaching out to children in a very personal and revolutionary fashion. While most adults still clung to segregation, Rogers had embraced the concept that God is color-blind.

After graduating from high school, Rogers enrolled at Dartmouth College in Hanover, New Hampshire. The Ivy League setting seemed perfect for the intellectual and thoughtful student. Yet after two years Rogers took a huge leap of faith, leaving New England and its familiar confines for Rollins College in Winter Park, Florida. There, while studying music composition, he met Sara Joanne Byrd, the woman he married in 1952.

Armed with a degree, Rogers moved to New York City to seek work in the television industry. The move shocked many of his friends because Rogers had often complained that TV was little more than a crass wasteland of violence and pratfalls. He felt that the medium's potential was great but that no one seemed to care to use television as a positive teaching tool for children or adults. So it seemed out of character for the very disciplined Rogers to beg producers to allow him to learn every facet of this new entertainment.

Rogers later explained the disconnect between his emotions and his vocation. "I went into television because I hated it so, and I thought there was some way of using this fabulous instrument to be of nurture to those who would watch and listen." He wanted to change the course of American broadcasting, but as things turned out, it took him almost two decades to get the chance to put his own ideas on a national stage.

His first job was at NBC, which employed him only because he had a music degree and they needed someone to help them with *NBC Opera Theater* and *Your Hit Parade*. After that he became the floor manager for *The Kate Smith Show* and then found a gig working with cowboy character actor Gabby Hayes, Roy Rogers' old sidekick. Hayes was developing a show aimed at the audience who loved his shenanigans in the old B westerns. That audience, of course, was made up of children.

Rogers thrived in the children's genre. He loved watching kids respond to live programming and had a wealth of ideas. Yet the commercial aspects of having to constantly pump products to pay the bills caused him to question the validity and value of most children's programs. While he was making a living and learning a great deal about the industry, he felt he was not living out a calling to serve God and often felt his time was wasted.

For several more years Rogers labored in this environment. Finally, all but burned out in commercial television, he moved back to Pittsburgh to work at WQED, the oldest public television station in the country. Yet while he produced original programming, he made another move, away from the studio, that clearly signaled his life was heading in a much different direction.

Soon after returning to his home state, Rogers entered Pittsburgh Theological Seminary. Even as a child, he had felt a call to become a minister. Yet with a wife and two children, he needed to earn a living, and that sharply cut into his ability to attend classes. Taking one course a semester, Rogers, now a television station executive, spent eight years out of the spotlight and behind the scenes in a public broadcasting station before finally earning his theology degree.

The leaders of the Presbyterian Church fully expected Fred to become a pastor; after all, that is why students spent years attending seminary. So as they interviewed the new graduate, they asked him what kind of role he felt most comfortable in as a worship leader, and who his favorite preachers were. In a quiet voice Rogers answered the questions, even telling a short story about a pastor he once heard who seemed lost in his delivery. And yet it was that preacher with his very simple sermon who touched his friends with just the message they needed to hear.

It was obvious that Rogers had given great thought to the type of preaching style that could make the greatest impact on a congregation. Better yet, with his calm demeanor and easy smile, he seemed the perfect embodiment of a young pastor. So the church leaders were shocked when he announced he had no desire to preach; instead he felt God had long been calling him into the world of television. Rogers believed that the Lord wanted him to use the lessons he had learned in life and in the classroom, coupling them with his experience in TV to create rich, meaningful programming that fed the spirits of children. In fact, he believed that God had set out a course—from Rogers' being bullied as a child, to his learning the piano, to his majoring in music composition and working in television—to bring him to this point. Needless to say, mouths were agape as the leaders of the denomination heard the man's unusual view of his calling.

It was 1962, and most denominations had little clue as to how to properly use television. The technique employed by church groups was to set up a camera in a sanctuary and point it at the preacher. The world of children's programming was all but unknown and rarely considered by Christians. And now Rogers was begging for a chance to change that view. Still not fully understanding his vision, the Presbyterian Church leadership granted Rogers his unusual and seemingly bizarre wish to pursue what he saw as his call, but the group provided no seed money.

Forced to turn back to the private sector to find support for his new venture, Rogers quickly discovered that few were interested in the preschool crowd. Scores of sponsors turned him down. Finally, to realize his dream, he had to become a "foreign missionary."

A year after completing seminary, thirty-five-year-old Rogers received an offer from the Canadian Broadcasting Corporation to develop a daily fifteen-minute television program aimed at young children. With little more than faith to guide him, Rogers moved his family north. For the next three years *Mister Rogers* was a hit with preschool kids. Using his soft voice and gentle manner, the host charmed kids and their parents alike. In the process, he developed little sets to illustrate his stories. Many of these, such as the trolley and the castle, later became part of his "neighborhood" when he moved the concept back to the United States three years later.

Back in Pittsburgh at WQED in 1966, Rogers produced *The Children's Corner* and, using phone calls, letters, and personal visits to cities up and down the East Coast, developed a loose affiliation of PBS stations known as the Eastern Educational Network. This small but growing team of stations in Pittsburgh, Boston, Washington, D.C., and New York City provided him with the opportunity to come back in front of the camera with a new program based on his successful Canadian kids' show. Finally, with funding in place, Rogers was getting a chance to invade the great TV wasteland with a program that embraced the ancient theme that it is better to live a sermon than speak one. His target audience, those who would be molded by his faith, were children.

In the weeks before *Mister Rogers' Neighborhood* was scheduled to kick off, the host asked his church family at the Sixth Presbyterian Church to pray for the program's success. He really believed that, even though the show would air on Public Broadcasting Stations, children would be able to feel God's presence in it.

Those who knew Rogers well were hardly surprised he was making calls and asking his friends to pray for the programming. Rogers had long believed in the power of prayer and often prayed for his friends. In fact, he rose each day at 5:30 and prayed for all those going through a difficult time. Although he was not in the pulpit, Rogers prayed and studied the Bible more than most preachers. Yet even those closest to him doubted that a PBS show aimed at preschoolers could make much of an impression on children who were being given large doses of violence on the tube daily. However, Rogers so believed that God's hand had been guiding his life to put him in this time and place that many prayed for a miracle.

On February 19, 1968, Rogers paused outside his Pittsburgh studio and stood in the cold wind. Bowing his head, he said a short, silent prayer he continued to repeat each day for more than three decades. "Dear God, let some word that is heard be yours." Though Rogers couldn't have guessed it then, God blessed this simple prayer by reshaping a generation.

Mister Rogers' Neighborhood was like nothing else on TV. Each episode began the same way. Mister Rogers came in singing the song "Won't You Be My Neighbor," pulled off his coat and dress shoes, slipped into sneakers and a sweater, and began a conversation with his audience. He always spoke as if there were only one person listening. Over the next thirty minutes he told stories, took his viewers on trips to places like a store or a train station, and introduced his special guests, many of them homemade puppets. In each carefully scripted program, he sought to make sure anyone who listened knew that his neighborhood was a place where each guest was always welcome and where they were always safe.

Every critic who viewed the show during its first few weeks saw it as hopelessly outdated. It was a relic from at least a generation before. It lacked energy and drive. It had no flash and there were no "wow" factors. They predicted that kids would tune it out before it had run a week. Yet the audience grew, and normally rambunctious children sat motionless for thirty minutes each day as if mesmerized by this hopelessly unhip host. Why would modern kids get so caught up in finding out how things like bulldozers or planes worked? Why would they give up colorful Disney animation for the unmoving pictures in the books Rogers read? Why would they find it so fascinating to watch him feed a goldfish? No one seemed to understand but Rogers.

Thinking back to his own childhood, he realized the importance of the quiet times. He knew what it meant to have a parent or a grandparent create a puppet or sing a song with you. He knew the feelings that went with being in a place that felt secure and safe, where there were no surprises or shocks. Most important, he knew that the only way to get these personal concepts across was to give them to children in a simple, direct fashion and in small doses. He realized that in a hurry-up world filled with noise and confusion, this type of programming was more important than ever.

In time Rogers developed themes for each week's series of broadcasts. One might be going to school, another learning how to use a new word. He would say things like, "Can you say *bus*?" And then when he had given his viewers a chance to say that word, he would add, "I knew you could do it." To three-, four-, and five-year-olds, many growing up in poverty or suffering from physical or verbal abuse, Rogers' constant praise meant the world. To thousands, his was the only gentle voice they heard all day, and his neighborhood was the only consistently peaceful place they ever visited.

Realizing that music resonated with little ones, Rogers began to write songs for his programs. These songs were little more than teaching aids for the lessons he was presenting. Rarely more than a verse and a chorus in length, so simple they could be memorized after just a few airings, the little songs were the first many children learned to sing. Best of all, each of these musical numbers had a theme that reinforced how special each individual is.

Because Rogers spoke directly and lovingly to kids in a language they could understand, millions felt as if he were their uncle or grandparent. Taking a trip to his neighborhood was like going to see that relative at their really special home. This spiritual connection made the show a success.

Less than a year after his first program aired, Rogers was asked to appear before the United States Senate Subcommittee on Communications. His goal was to gain support for the continued funding for PBS and the Corporation for Public Broadcasting. The senate was cutting taxes, and PBS funding was a prime target, so this was going to be a tough fight. Before entering the chambers,

Rogers said the prayer he repeated each day before entering his studio. Then he went into a place where he could not rely on a script. This was anything but a safe neighborhood for the TV host.

The chairman of the subcommittee, John O. Pastore, had no clue as to who Rogers was or what he did. All Pastore wanted to accomplish was to work through the testimony as quickly as he could. The senator was certain that there were much more important things on his agenda than dealing with a program aimed at preschoolers. Described as tough and ruthless, Pastore showed his swagger early as he cut the television host off just when he began to speak. After making sure everyone knew he was in charge, the elected official demanded to know what Rogers did on his program that was worth the taxpayers' support.

"This is what I give," Rogers quietly answered. "I give an expression of care every day to each child, to help him realize that he is unique. I end the program by saying, 'You've made this day a special day by just your being you. There's no person in the whole world like you, and I like you just the way you are.' I feel that if we in public television can only make it clear that feelings are mentioned and manageable, we will have done a great service."

Pastore grew strangely silent, shook his head, and replied, "I'm supposed to be a pretty tough guy. This is the first time I've had goose bumps in the last two days. Looks like you just earned the $20 million [for PBS]."

Fueled by this public acceptance of his calling, Rogers went back to his hometown and expanded his program, not through visual gimmicks but by videotaped visits to places like children's hospitals, police stations, doctors' offices, schools, and fire stations. He quietly explained how things work and why some things that might appear scary are not. There were no hidden messages in his presentations, just wisdom wrapped in direct language that children could understand. In his calm world, he made an often scary world look inviting.

Rogers was two years into *Mister Rogers' Neighborhood* when his pet goldfish died. Knowing this act might fuel a deep and lasting lesson, he dealt with that death on the air rather than simply and privately replacing the original fish. Over the years he tackled other tough subjects by presenting gentle stories that centered on ways to endure and deal with illness, divorce, and disappointment. So while other "cool" shows avoided the hard stuff of life, he confronted it in a way children could absorb.

In 1983 the ABC miniseries *The Day After* presented in very graphic visuals the aftereffects of a nuclear war. Many adult viewers of this program were so badly shaken they could not sleep for days. Rogers knew that some of the tiny kids who watched his program had seen some of these scenes as well. If their parents couldn't handle it, then how could the children cope?

At the conclusion of Friday's episode the week *The Day After* aired, Rogers sang a new song on the program. Kids who were expecting his usual rendition of "Good Feeling" were drawn closer to the screen as he sang an unfamiliar lullaby, "Peace and Quiet." This was followed by the words from Isaiah 2:4: "And they shall beat their swords into plowshares, and their spears into pruning hooks: nation shall not lift up sword against nation, neither shall they learn war any more."

The letters that came in over the next weeks showed that while children had embraced his message and felt good about it, it was the parents watching the show with them who most deeply appreciated Rogers' wishes of peace and hope. In a unique way, he had brought families together and caused them to think about the wisdom found in the Bible. Letters he received afterward revealed that many of these same families had later picked up their own Bibles and reread those same words with their children.

Almost a decade later, when other children's shows avoided mentioning the Gulf War, Mister Rogers assured his viewers they would be safe in his neighborhood. He also got parents and grand-parents involved in making sure children understood that they were secure in their homes as well. Rogers knew that bad news affects kids, and he understood how to address that news in a way that made it seem less scary. Few of the nation's greatest politicians had been able to do that with adults, much less kids.

Within a decade of the debut of *Mister Rogers' Neighborhood*, the host was a national institution. In 1990 his Oldsmobile was stolen. But the car was returned to the same spot a few days later. When the thief discovered he had taken Mister Rogers' car, he was overcome with guilt. Not only did he not touch any personal items inside, but he also left a note that read, "I am sorry. I didn't know this car belonged to you."

More than any person on television, Rogers so represented honesty and goodness that even criminals did not feel right taking advantage of him. One high school student admitted to a newsman that he felt the host was incredibly uncool, but he then added, "You know, I'd trust that man with anything I had."

In 1997 the *Daytime Emmy Awards Show* presented Fred Rogers with the Lifetime Achievement Award. Stepping to the microphone, Rogers said, "All of us have special ones who have loved us into being. Would you just take, along with me, ten seconds to think of the people who have helped you become who you are?"

Esquire magazine covered the event, and writer Tom Junod was as stunned as everyone else. The journalist wrote about that moment, "Then he lifted his wrist, looked at the audience, looked at his watch, and said, 'I'll watch the time.' There was, at first, a small whoop from the crowd, a giddy, strangled hiccup of laugh-ter, as people realized that he wasn't kidding.... Then tears fell, gathering like rain leaking down a crystal chandelier. And Mister Rogers finally looked up from his watch and said softly, 'May God be with you.'" It was a moment that none there would ever forget, a dynamic sermon in only a few words.

In the last few years of his life, Rogers was constantly sought out and asked about the secret of his success. He explained, "My whole approach in broadcasting has always been you are an important person just the way you are. You can make healthy decisions."

In his office hung a framed line written in French from Antonie de Saint-Exupery's *The Little Prince*. Translated, it said, "What is essential is invisible to the eye." Rogers understood that God is with all of us; he also realized that children can see this invisible, essential truth when adults miss it altogether. His program revealed this truth in a way that opened up the real "God world" of peace and love to kids.

Yet more than anything else, he understood the nature of what can be learned when we are calm and quiet. He once sent out Christmas cards that said, "May you be blessed with moments of silence and hope at Christmas and always." Prayer, Bible study, and positive interaction with individuals were where he found this Christmas hope. And he wrapped what he learned from his life in a wonderful package that he freely gave out every day of the year. In many ways he was very much like Jesus, a person who really did live out the message of compassion of the one he knew as Savior.

The fact that many others saw Christ's hope in his actions was proven over and over again. In the mid-1980s, when thirty-year-old actress Lauren Tewes accidentally tuned in to *Mister Rogers' Neighborhood*, her life was a mess. At the time, the television star was hooked on cocaine. She later told her friends and fans that it was Rogers' calming influence that she needed to turn her life around. Imagine finding the resources to kick a drug habit on a children's show aimed at preschoolers. Yet in his simple, direct way, Rogers allowed kids, as well as the child buried inside adults, to feel, to see, and to absorb lessons they would really understand much later. Ms.

Tewes was one of millions who discovered the power and universal nature of the faith Rogers presented each day on his program.

Rogers told CNN reporter Jeff Greenfield, "[My goal was] to look at the television camera and present as much love as you possibly could to a person who might feel that he or she needs it." One fan, trying to sum up the power of Rogers' work and faith, wrote, "In the twentieth century, he ranks with Martin Luther King and Gandhi. Nobody knows how much peace and love he sowed."

One of his coworkers added, "There was a point in every child's life where he was the nicest person on television." Maybe even the nicest man in the world.

Tim Reeves, a former writer and a partner with the Neiman Group wrote this after Rogers' death: "I have been privileged in my life to meet many great people. As a journalist and as a government official, I have talked with three presidents, dozens of governors and scores of celebrities and CEOs.... But I have known only one person who ranks as one of the truly great people in American history. That man is Fred Rogers."

Rogers, with his gentle ways, embodied unconditional love. He used that love on television like no one ever has. And without his even saying "Jesus" on the air, people somehow knew that was who he followed.

In 2000 Rogers told Wendy Zoba of *Christianity Today*, "I think about heaven, it is a state in which we are so greatly loved that there is no fear and doubt and disillusionment and anxiety. It is where people really do look at you with those eyes of Jesus."

Fred Rogers died on February 27, 2003. The president noted his passing, and his memorial service drew almost three thousand mourners, including David Hartman, Teresa Heinz Kerry, philanthropist Elsie Hillman, PBS president Pat Mitchell, *Arthur* creator Marc Brown, and *The Very Hungry Caterpillar* author-illustrator Eric Carle. At the gathering, those who eulogized him remembered

Rogers' love of children and music, as well as endearing quirks and his faith. It was this faith that somehow changed them. So how could this man who never gave an invitation call or preached a sermon touch so many lives with such great faith?

For starters, he lived as Francis of Assisi called every Christian to live. His life was his sermon. He said, "Those of us in broadcasting have a special calling to give whatever we feel is the most nourishing that we can for our audience. We are servants of those who watch and listen." Though the program was not religious, thousands wrote to him declaring they saw Jesus in his words and actions.

Reporting on his death on NBC, Bob Faw said, "The real Mister Rogers never preached, never mentioned God. He never had to." Fred Rogers had a faith so strong, most mortals could not begin to comprehend its lasting power and impact, but generations of kids are better for having grown up in his faith-based neighborhood.

13

NICK VUJICIC
Living without Limitation

He was just fifteen years old, a handsome young man blessed with piercing eyes, a charismatic smile, and a wonderful personality. He was funny, charming, and intelligent. Yet few noticed any of these special elements that should have defined the teen. Something else caught everyone's attention, something dramatic, unusual, and to some, horrifying. Nick Vujicic was born without limbs. He had no arms and no legs. Rather than being the most popular person at his school, he was most often looked upon as the "freak."

In another day and time, the world would have offered Nick only three alternatives. The first would have been death, as most babies born with such a condition were left to die. The second would have been to spend his entire life locked in an institution that existed only to shield the normal from those with horrific disabilities. The final option would have been to make a meager living working in a carnival sideshow.

Yet in the 1990s, even with so many doors having been opened for the handicapped, Nick's options were still few. So by almost everyone but his own family, he had been written off long before he could speak his first word. After all, how could this child ever have the opportunity to make a lasting, meaningful, positive mark on the world? It seemed so obviously impossible. So he was forever doomed to be one of "God's mistakes."

In his dreams, Nick had arms and legs. He could run, dance, and play soccer. When he slept, he was the kid who was always leading others along the walkway of life. Yet in a dramatic way, the morning always brought the reality of what he was back to life. It seemed that reality was never as sweet as his dreams.

Nick couldn't just jump out of bed; he had to roll and land on his single two-toed foot. He then had to contort his body just to hop to his door, which he opened by pulling on a rope cord with his mouth. If you spent five minutes in his world, it would be obvious that nothing came easy for the boy. Nothing could be taken for granted either. Even in his family's house, which was remodeled for his special needs, life was a constant struggle. Yet his life at home was easy compared with what he faced in the real world.

The teen years are often a torturous experience, but for Nick they were at times a living hell. Every day he was ridiculed, bullied, or ignored. Many didn't approach him for fear that his mind was as incomplete as his body. Perceptions governed everything in his life. It was as if he had a target pasted to his chest and people couldn't wait to get their chance to shoot their insults or offer their pity. How many times did he overhear, "Why is he out in public?" or "It's a shame that someone like that was ever born." So from the start, Nick was the ultimate outsider, and nothing would change that fact.

Nick's father and mother had been immigrants to Australia. They had come "down under" with the goal of starting a church for the many people from Eastern Europe who had moved to the outback. Their faith had taken them halfway around the globe, and that faith would lead the couple through the tough times after their first son was born.

Yet sometimes they even wondered about God. They constantly taught that God was love. Yet the question that rolled over and over in their minds was why, if the Lord is so loving, had he made Nick this way?

Nick also struggled with his faith. Even though he believed in the existence of God, he had a very tough time accepting Jesus as his Savior. Why ask God for grace when he hadn't even given you arms or legs, much less hope and compassion? It was far easier to blame the Supreme Being than ask him for help.

For years Nick had both longed for God and pushed him away. Yet as he matured into his teens, as his options grew fewer and fewer and his prospects for life seemed so dramatically limited, he turned to the book his father treasured. Even though Nick had looked for answers in the Bible on many occasions and never found them, maybe now it would be different.

Finally, in John 9, Nick discovered the answer. In this passage, Jesus is confronted by a blind man, and his disciples demand to know why the man was born with such a condition. As he read, Nick was amazed by the Lord's response: "Neither hath this man sinned, nor his parents: but that the works of God should be made manifest in him" (v. 3).

It seemed to Nick that the man had been given the condition so the works of God could be revealed in the way he approached his life. In other words, it wasn't about what the world thought of him; it was about his personal attitude.

Seizing upon this promise like a drowning man grabbing a life preserver, Nick began to wonder if maybe God could reveal something special by using this child without limbs. As he fully gave himself to the Lord to use as God saw fit, a warmth flowed through Nick's small body. For the very first time, he truly believed that he was born for a purpose and that it was simply a matter of finding out what the purpose was. He knew the world still might see him as a freak, but he was also sure God didn't. And that was all that mattered.

Fully embracing faith changed Nick deeply. No more did he wallow in sorrow, no more did he spend hours wishing for things that could not happen, no more did he dare God to come to him and prove himself by healing his incomplete body. Now he embraced the Lord he had once pushed away. This was a huge leap of faith for a boy who had once spent much of his spare time praying to die.

At the age of eight Nick had contemplated for weeks trying to come up with a method for a person without limbs to commit suicide. He finally decided his best route was to ask someone to place him on a high countertop where he could then do a dive to the floor and land on his head. He thought this might break his neck and end the pain of living in a world where he was constantly abused. Now, feeling the promise of God's grace in his life, he was so glad he had never acted on that plan.

As he counted his blessings, Nick suddenly found many other things to be grateful for. He was smart, quick-witted, and had a great family. And maybe the best of his blessings was the gift of being able to breathe. Yes, now after finding saving grace, he knew that even his very difficult life was a special gift to treasure. Being alive and different was far better than being dead and forgotten. And if he had been born into a different family in a different place and time, that might well have been his fate.

The Vujicic family had emigrated from Serbia in the Australian winter of 1982. They settled in Melbourne, started a church, and anxiously looked forward to the December birth of their first child. Over the months leading up to that blessed event, the couple had an ultrasound, as well as all other suggested tests. To the physicians, the baby appeared healthy and normal.

On the morning of December 4, Mrs. Vujicic went into labor. A few hours later she gave birth. The doctor and nurses grew strangely silent as the boy came into the world. As his mother glanced down at the baby, ready to praise God for the sound of her son's crying voice, she too saw the strange, incomplete creature she had carried for nine months. When the nurse offered to allow her to hold the child, the new mother declined. In a quiet voice she begged them, "Please, take him away."

Nick's father was brought to his knees when he heard the news. He didn't know what to do or say. Tears filled his eyes. Even as a pastor who believed in a loving God, he questioned, "What have we done to deserve this? Why has God done this to me?" As he inventoried his life, he found no answers.

The church the family had started was equally devastated. This child, who had been prayed for by each of the members, who would be the first new baby to bless this congregation, was a freak of nature. Many could not even go to the hospital to see him in the nursery. Others kept asking, "If God truly is a God of love, then why would he let something this bad happen to not just anyone but these incredible and dedicated Christian people?" So instead of celebrating, the church members went into a state of mourning. Over and over they moaned, "This poor couple will never again have a normal life. What a burden has been placed on them. How could God do this?"

Within hours of the birth, Reverend Vujicic came out of his shocked state long enough to hold the child in his arms. As he stared at his son, the man had to acknowledge that the boy really did have a beautiful face, but with no arms or legs and only a tiny appendage for a foot barely protruding from where his thigh should have been, it seemed obvious that the boy would not live long. When the doctors took the child away for a series of tests, Vujicic fully expected the results to show a myriad of internal problems to go with the boy's obvious birth defects. Yet the medical procedures proved that other than his lack of limbs, the child was in perfect health. So he would live, but what kind of life would he have?

Many of the professionals at the hospital suggested the baby be placed in an institution. They argued that it would be best for the parents and the boy. Yet after their shock wore off, the Vujicics saw Nick as more than just an ill-formed tiny human; he was a test of their faith. How they responded to this situation would show others how they really viewed the gift of life. Hence, as did millions of other parents, they bundled the baby up in their arms and took him to the nursery they had prepared at their modest home. They were going to do everything in their power to provide this strange little boy with a wonderful and loving home.

"Understandably," Nick explained, "my parents had strong concerns and fears of what kind of life I'd be able to lead. God provided them strength, wisdom, and courage through those early years."

Early on, that heavenly inspiration provided the child with not only a good home but also a great frame of mind. While he couldn't walk, his parents did teach him to hop on his one foot. They also devised new ways for him to use his mouth for everything from playing with toys to putting on his clothes. As best they could, they made him self-sufficient. More important, they didn't hide him away. They took him to the market, on trips, and to church. They showed no shame in his obvious handicap and constantly pointed out how bright he was. They were proud of the unique victories and accomplishments they saw in Nick's adapting to life with no limbs.

But the Vujicics knew that for the boy to really live, he would have to make his way into the real world, one they couldn't control. For Nick to reach his potential, at six he would have to join other children in school. Yet this simple and expected passage of life was blocked for Nick, as the bridge between his world and the world of normal children had never been built. The law in Australia did not allow Nick to be integrated into a mainstream school because of his physical disability.

Rather than simply accept the time-honored system that separated the "normal" children from those who were different, Nick's mother opted to fight. In letters and spoken words she took on the school laws, showing that while it was true her son had physical limitations, he was mentally sound and therefore should not be placed in special education classes. She made the effort to show educators that Nick was well ahead of most children his age in reading and comprehension. His verbal skills were also excellent. Why, she argued, should his brain be limited and his potential denied just because he had to hold a pencil between his toes?

As Mrs. Vujicic pushed, others joined in the fight. Scores of youngsters in the Melbourne area were being shut out of school simply because they looked different. These otherwise normal children were being shunned by a prejudice that had no place in the second half of the twentieth century. Suddenly thousands were screaming that it was time to change this archaic practice. After months of wrangling, the school system gave in. The Vujicic's firstborn would be allowed to attend regular classes.

The boy with no limbs became the first child with a major disability to become a part of the mainstream education programs in his hometown. Most were rooting against him. They argued that having such a radically different child in the classroom would prove a distraction for other students. Yet the real reason for their lobbying against Nick was that most simply couldn't bring themselves to accept this strange boy as a peer to their own children.

In 1932 Hollywood director Todd Browning sensed society's great apprehension of men and women with conditions similar to Nick's. Coming off his successful hit horror film *Dracula*, Browning created a motion picture in which normal people were evil and mean and those with physical deformities were compassionate and caring. When *Freaks* premiered, audiences were shocked. Many cities banned the movie, and many churches led protests against it. In truth, people simply could not face their own prejudices. They considered themselves good people, yet while watching *Freaks*, they found themselves rooting for the normal people even though the characters were demonically evil. The motion picture held up a mirror that even most Christians of the era didn't want to look into for fear of the spiritual imperfections they would see.

Now, in 1988, the battle was again being fought, this time not in a movie theater but in a school. And once more, many of those who considered themselves normal were rooting against a person they considered a freak of nature. The pressure was on Nick to perform, not just for himself but for all the others who had been shut out by the system.

Not surprisingly, Nick was a dynamic student. He excelled at every facet of classroom work. Yet his peers reacted to his presence much as did the normal characters in the movie *Freaks*. They bullied and teased him. Some tried to hurt him. A few knocked him down, laughed at him, and called him names. Those who didn't pick on the boy ignored him altogether. It was this sting of not even being allowed to exist, of having others try to erase his image and form, that hurt the worst. The once extroverted boy drew deeply inside a protective shell. As he grew to hate school, he also grew to hate himself.

"Many times I felt depressed and angry because I couldn't change the way I was," Nick explained. "In Sunday school I learned that God loves us all and that he cares for us deeply. At that stage in my childhood, I could understand his love to a point. But, as you can imagine, I still got hung up on that fact that if he really loved me, why did he make me like this? I wondered if I'd done something wrong and began to feel certain that this must be true. Otherwise, I thought, God wouldn't have made me the only weird one out of all the kids at school."

By his eighth birthday the boy was ready to give up. He was now old enough to see just how different he was and realize what a burden he was on his mother and father, as well as on his younger brother and sister. He wanted to die. He could see no future or hope for anyone who was born like him.

In church Nick had been taught that God can work miracles. Nothing is beyond his reach. So each night, the boy prayed that his heavenly Father would give him what his parents could not: real arms and legs, real hands, and real feet. Surely, if God truly loved him, he would do this for him. Then the children at school would see him for what he really was—a very special person with dreams and ideas. Yet the miracle never came.

Giving up on growing new limbs, one day Nick looked in the mirror. In his reflection he sought to find one element of his being he could cling to as being special. What he found staring back was a boy who had been blessed with beautiful eyes. They were expressive, interesting, and deep. They reflected a person who might well have been made in God's image. After all, God didn't need hands to form the world. He didn't need legs to survey his universe. So maybe Nick really was a reflection of God's heart. That concept kept him going on days when everything and everyone seemed to line up against him. Then, when he discovered the passage about the blind man in John 9, his self-concept really began to change.

Nick latched on to a notion that "God won't let anything happen to you unless he has a good purpose for it." For the teen, the problem was finding that purpose. Surely, it had to be more than showing people he could surf the internet with his foot, kick a soccer ball, swim, play a synthesizer, shave himself, comb his hair, and even brush his teeth. Almost anyone could do that, so what did that prove? How could God use that to make life worthwhile? There had to be more.

"I started to develop attitudes and values which helped me overcome these challenging times. I knew that I was different but on the inside I was just like everyone else. There were many times when I felt so low that I wouldn't go to school just so I didn't have to face all the negative attention. I was encouraged by my parents to ignore them and to try to start making friends by just talking with some kids. Soon the students realized that I was just like them, and starting there God kept on blessing me with new friends."

Nick first saw his real potential when his school brought in a special speaker. The young man was an orphan and spoke of how difficult it had been growing up in a world where he felt connected to no one. As a boy, the speaker explained, he had felt intense loneliness and fear. Nick believed this man was talking directly to him. This was also his life story. As he considered the joy of knowing he was not alone in his doubts and sense of isolation, he began to realize that there must be millions of others who felt the same way. Maybe Nick had a message that would resonate with them just as this speaker's words had touched his heart.

A few weeks later, at the age of seventeen, Nick spoke to his church about his life. Afterward men and women who had always seemed scared by his mere presence came up to give him a hug. Within weeks other churches and a few schools had asked him to address groups. He found that his message especially hit home with two very unique groups. The first was the elderly, who often believed their best days were behind them. Many of these seniors had given up on even speaking in Sunday school classes because they felt no one wanted to hear their thoughts. Yet through Nick's message about God using anyone who would just go to where he leads, many of these forgotten souls again got active with a wide variety of groups. They began to touch others with an optimistic hope.

The other group deeply moved by his message was teens. Nick was shocked at how many of his peers had low self-esteem. Many who came up and visited with him after his talks were suicidal. They had been rejected by their families and classmates so many times, they had given up. Thus drugs and alcohol appealed to them in ways their parents couldn't understand. Yet when they heard Nick speak of God using him because he was different, it gave them hope and the courage to try again. At this point Nick began to realize that what he gave people was the ability to believe in second chances.

As he plunged into college, working on a double major in the business department, he continued to speak. He now formed his message by combining his own experiences with his new understanding of the inadequacies of seemingly normal people.

"If we went by the world's definition of who I'm supposed to be because I look weird," he told thousands, "then surely this guy can't have a productive life. Surely he doesn't have a sense of humor. Surely he can't love life. We stereotype people in this world. And so if the world thinks you're not good enough, it's a lie. Get a second opinion."

By the time Nick graduated from college, he had spoken to more than a hundred thousand people. Yet even as he began his career in stock trading and real estate development, offers continued to pour in, asking him to speak everywhere from churches to conventions. And those requests were now coming from all around the world.

As he traveled the globe, many began to videotape his message. Soon, thanks to YouTube, tens of millions were watching this small man on their computers. There he was, balancing on a table and encouraging people to have faith in God and in themselves. Over and over, troubled teens went online to hear Nick beg them to live a life without limits, and millions grasped this message and changed their outlook on life. If Nick believed he was special and if he had the courage to dream, then they had no excuses not to dream too.

Soon, as the web spelled out his optimistic message to every corner of the globe, Nick became one of the most popular Christian voices in the world. Within two years after graduating from college, Nick had visited twenty nations and spoken to more than two million people in person and tens of millions more via the internet.

In Africa, AIDS orphans picked him up and lifted him into the air as they sang and praised God. They saw this deformed man as one of them. If he could achieve, so could they. If he believed in God, so could they. This scene was repeated in hundreds of other places, with people of all races joining in Nick's celebration of life. Here was a man with no limbs living out the Great Commission of Christ in ways few "normal" individuals would have believed possible.

Beginning his own nonprofit, inspirational arm of faith, known as Life without Limbs, Nick sought to expand his work to reach even more struggling souls. The very thing that had once so limited his world and potential was now allowing him to go to every part of the earth and inspire people to reach higher than they had ever thought they could.

"Our life is the best testimony we can give. Always be open to the way God wants to use us. When you fall down, you have to get up; it should be impossible for me to get up, but I can. But you and I can't do this on our own. It is a lie that you need to do this life on your own. You can talk to him; he wants to be with you. He will pull you through. 'My grace is sufficient, my strength is made perfect in your weakness.'"

When asked if he still prays for God to work a miracle and grow the arms and legs he has never had, Nick always smiles and answers, "That's where I am. That's the freedom and victory I have. I believe in a God who can do all things, but if he chooses not to give me arms and legs, I know it's for the better. And I may not understand it, but all I need to know is that he's going to carry me through, that there is a purpose for it."

Nick's mission has evolved into encouraging people not to give up, into being a living example that struggle leads to strength. And he now realizes that the way he was born is what has made his incredible work possible. "It turns out having no arms and legs has gotten me into some doors I would not have been able to walk through."

Nick, who was once angry at God for allowing him to be deformed, now seeks to point the spotlight away from himself and to the Lord. "Now that I've found my purpose in Christ, there's no greater satisfaction than being able to glorify him and speak to people about God and his love for them and encourage them to fulfill their dreams.

"I believe that if you have the desire and passion to do something, and if it's God's will, you will achieve it in good time. As humans, we continually put limits on ourselves for no reason at all!

What's worse is putting limits on God, who can do all things. We put God in a box. The awesome thing about the power of God is that if we want to do something for God, instead of focusing on our capability, concentrate on our availability, for we know that it is God through us and we can't do anything without him. Once we make ourselves available for God's work, guess whose capabilities we rely on? God's!"

To millions who don't know him, Nick is still a freak. To many he is still a sideshow attraction. Yet when he is given a chance to speak to those who so fear his abnormalities, they find a person who can show them more about God and their potential than anyone who can walk this earth.

Nick was a boy who, if he had had other parents and his condition had been revealed before birth, probably would have been aborted. He was a boy who, if he had had other parents, surely would have been locked away in a facility for the severely handicapped. He was a boy who was shunned by his classmates and unwanted by his school. Yet he has become a man who survived all the rejection to find that he must have been made in the image of God, because millions have now come to see God thanks to his message.

Everywhere he visits, Nick quotes this verse: "I can do all things through Christ who strengthens me" (Philippians 4:13). And as if that message were not enough, he adds, "No arms, no legs, no worries!" That defines walking with faith. That defines Nick Vujicic. That defines a hero.

14

NICHOLAS OF MYRA
Giving His Life

The roots of Santa Claus are not found in the snows of the North Pole but were planted by third-century acts of charity in a region we now know as Turkey. Ancient Christian writings indicate that the real person on whom the famous Christmas elf was based was a wisp of a man, slightly built, and probably little more than five feet tall.

As a cardinal in the church, Nicholas of Myra, like Santa, would have been seen in flowing red robes, and early Christian art does reveal that late in his life Nicholas might well have had a white beard and balding head. Yet what made this church pioneer a model for the Christmas icon of goodwill was not his physical appearance but rather what was so freely displayed in his heart. It was Nicholas's giving spirit, great compassion, and unending generosity that inspired a holiday legend now known by billions around the globe.

Nicholas was born in the Greek city of Patara around 270 AD. The son of a businessman named Theophanes and his wife, Nonna, the child's earliest years were spent in Myra, a bustling financial center filled with shops, cottage industries, and schools. As a port on the Mediterranean Sea, in the middle of sea lanes that linked Egypt, Greece, and Rome, Myra was a destination for traders, fishermen, and merchant sailors. Spawned by the spirit of both the city's Greek heritage and the ruling Roman government, cultural endeavors such as art, drama, and music were mainstays of everyday life. On the surface, Myra appeared to be an ideal place to live and a wonderful city in which to raise a bright child like

Nicholas. Yet underneath the sophisticated, urbane atmosphere was a much darker side.

As is often the case with centers of commerce, Myra was home not just to the highest elements of modern social culture but also to all of the world's vices. The early Christian church, which did have a presence in the city, was often at odds with the debauchery that abounded through every level of the social structure. But the influence of that religious community paled compared with the power of the Roman gods. Gambling, prostitution, and smuggling not only were common but were very much out in the open. More troubling to the clergy, Christians often took part in most of the local celebrations and enthusiastically embraced the depravity that was so much a part of the city's heritage.

Therefore even as a very young boy, Nicholas was exposed to the sinful nature of the local culture. Yet this exposure was tempered by his parents, committed Christians who constantly showed their faith to their only son not just through their words but also through their actions. They gave to missionary work and helped in local efforts to feed the poor. Theophanes and Nonna also took Nicholas to church services and enrolled him in Christian classes on theology and history.

Christian young people in Myra were taught *The Didache*, an early guide to Christian living. This text asked believers to fully embrace the Lord's two greatest commandments: to love God with all your heart and to love your neighbor as yourself. These lessons had a great impact on Nicholas. Even as a teen, he took a part of his allowance and shared it with poor children who did not have enough to eat. Yet the act which really set the boy apart began with a family friend's business failure.

In the weeks that followed, the man and his three daughters lost everything, including their home, and were forced to move to one of the slums just outside the city. With no money for food and unable to cope with watching his girls suffer, in an act of desperation the father began to negotiate with local brothel owners. He was seeking to sell his oldest daughter into sexual slavery to provide for the two younger children. By sacrificing one, he felt he could at least save the others.

When Nicholas became aware of the situation, he felt a call to action. The night before the girl was to be sold, Nicholas went to the family's home, waited for the lights to go out, and tossed a bag of gold through an open window. The boy vanished before the father could open the door to see who had provided them with such a great gift.

Where did a teenager get the gold? Logic provides the only possible answer. Nicholas must have either gone on the mission at the request of his parents or asked them if there was a way they could help the family. It is likely the money came from his father. Yet no matter who suggested the action or provided the funds, this act of kindness would have been an example of the family's devotion to Christ's teachings. And it would not just be a one-time act of charity.

The money provided by Nicholas lasted the family more than a year. When it ran out and the father was again contemplating selling one of his daughters, another bag of gold was secretly delivered in the night. A year later the youth returned again, but this time he was caught. The father was overcome with emotion when he saw that the person who had provided him with the lifeline was a boy.

Wiping away his tears, he hugged Nicholas and asked, "Why did you give us these gifts?"

The response was direct and simple: "Because you needed them."

Shaking his head, the man begged to know something that had been troubling him since the first bag of gold was quietly tossed into his home. "But why didn't you let us know who you were?"

Nicholas's answer would become the foundation for the legend that is still celebrated each Christmas season. "Because it's good to give and have only God know about it." The quiet, unannounced visits by "Santa Claus" still embrace this form of modest and unrewarded giving.

Though these acts of charity overwhelmed the failed businessman, Nicholas's three trips to the slum village paled when compared with what he did when confronted by the greatest tragedy a child can experience. In the midst of deep grief his life's mission would come into focus, and through that mission his name is still remembered to this day.

Nicholas was in his midteens when his parents died, probably the result of one of several plagues that hit the area during this period. The uncle he was named for, a priest, was placed in charge of the grieving boy.

As the two prayed for understanding, Nicholas was overcome with a sense of urgency to live out the lessons taught in his own home. He felt the best way to memorialize the ideals for which his parents stood was to take his considerable inheritance, cash it into Roman coins, and give all he had to the poorest families in the region.

Satisfied that his act had both honored his parents and his Lord, he then committed himself to Christian study. He felt that if he learned more about God, he could live more like Christ. As he plunged into academics, he was first tutored by his uncle and later attended school in the monastery Holy Sion. After completing his studies, he gave his life to full-time Christian service.

Nicholas probably entered the priesthood before reaching his twenties. The duties that fell to him during this period were anything but pleasant. The life of the once wealthy boy was now filled with poverty and trials. Under the Roman emperors Diocletian and Maximian, Christians were hunted and persecuted. Those who would not abandon their faith were often tortured, some even executed.

As a church leader in Myra, Nicholas was jailed. Yet unlike many who found the rat-infested prisons too much to bear, he saw confinement as an opportunity to share the gospel with fellow prisoners and even guards. Taking inspiration from the letters of the apostle Paul, Nicholas encouraged those outside the walls to continue to pray, support the work, and look to the Lord for strength. For ten long years the persecution of Christians continued throughout the Roman Empire, and the priest never flinched.

After his release, Nicholas oversaw a period of rebuilding in Myra. He devoted most of his energies to feeding the poor, locating shelter for the displaced and homeless, and finding families for those orphaned during the decade-long persecutions. Only when he felt sure that his flock was secure did he make a pilgrimage to Egypt and Palestine to further his own education.

On the journey back to Myra a powerful storm hit the ship on which Nicholas had booked passage. The sailors sought out the priest, explaining that unless conditions improved, the vessel would capsize. Nicholas stood on the deck, and with crying men gathered around him and fierce winds all but overturning the ship, he lifted his hands to the heavens and asked the Lord to protect these humble sailors. Within minutes the storm had passed, the seas became calm, and a crew of new converts bowed to thank God for his protection.

When the boat docked at Myra, word of the miracle quickly spread across the community. Within hours, scores of seafaring men made their way to the church Nicholas led. Each asked the priest to bless them before they headed off to often unfriendly waters. As the weeks became months and the story of salvation during a storm spread across Europe, more and more sailors sought out Nicholas. Within a year the little man had become the unofficial pastor of all who worked the Mediterranean waters. To this day, sailors still speak of the power Nicholas has over the sea's angry waves.

Due to the strength he had shown while in prison, as well as the faith he had lived during his sea voyage, Nicholas would have surely gained the office of bishop during his lifetime. But because of a series of unique circumstances, he was one of the few elected to that office before his thirtieth birthday.

After the former bishop's death, seated bishops gathered, as prescribed by church law, to select the next bishop for Myra. During the conclave, the most respected member of the counsel heard a voice in the night telling him to watch the doors of the church the next morning. This voice informed the bishop that the first man to enter St. Martin's Church whose given name was Nicholas was the man God had ordained to lead Myra.

After this bishop shared his dream with the other bishops, they all retired to the church, where they asked the name of each man who entered. After an hour the young priest who had come to mean so much to seamen walked through the entry. When the group inquired as to his name, he replied, "I am Nicholas."

The head bishop stepped toward him, grabbed his hand, and announced, "Nicholas, servant and friend of God, for your holiness you shall be bishop of this place." The surprised young man was then brought into the church and immediately consecrated the new bishop of Myra.

Perhaps because of the loss of his own parents, Nicholas had always felt a need to reach out to the next generation. In his new position, he centered even more of his work on kids. He spent a good portion of his day teaching and sharing clothing and food with the children of the poorest families in the area around Myra. Because of the gentle way he expressed his compassion and love, and because he often was seen carrying a bag filled with candy and gifts, it is hardly surprising that whenever he ventured out in public, Nicholas always seemed to have scores of children clinging to his red robes and following in his footsteps. Due to his work, the bishop quickly emerged as the face of God in the vicinity of Myra. His popularity was unrivaled.

Due to Nicholas's power with local citizens, Roman officials often sought out his advice in matters of state. The influence he gained through honest and respected council with these men allowed him to push agendas of faith and charity. Thus pagan temples were condemned, new churches constructed, and government-sponsored charity work initiated.

At such meetings as the Council of Nicaea, Nicholas spoke passionately for the establishment of Christianity as the official religion of Rome. He strongly believed that by putting Christ at the center of the Roman Empire, church missionaries would acquire official power and protection to better reach the lost throughout all of Europe. He also argued that if Rome were considered a Christian state, then the government would feel compelled to do much more for the poor people. Considering that a church was later built by the Roman emperor Justinian I and named for Nicholas, even though change did not come quickly, the clergyman certainly must have scored some points during those meetings with Roman officials. There seems to be little doubt they were inspired by his honesty and zeal.

The respect Nicholas was afforded in Rome and the power he quietly wielded could be clearly seen on another occasion, when the bishop listened to the confession of a prisoner about to be executed. Convinced the man was not guilty of the capital offense, he stood between the condemned prisoner and the gallows, demanding a new trial. If another priest had attempted to stop the edicts of the courts, the Roman leaders of Myra would have simply pushed him to one side. But Nicholas was the hero not just of sailors but also of thousands who had felt his compassionate hand. So when he spoke, a mob quickly formed and stood with him.

When ordered to stand down and let the executioner do his duty, the bishop refused. With thousands looking on, it became a matter of who would blink first. With God behind him and with the knowledge that he was protecting an innocent life, Nicholas did not budge. He called for Christians to protect this man who could no longer protect himself. In this case the defender of the faith won the battle, and the man was retried and proven innocent.

The bishop continued to work for the underprivileged and unrepresented poor in the matter of taxes. When local leaders did nothing to ease the burden of government taxation, Nicholas rode to the emperor's palace to spell out what the high tax rates were doing to the people of Myra. What Nicholas requested had already been addressed by countless other leaders throughout Europe, but Constantine gave in to the bishop when he had not given in to the others. Now, thanks to the way Nicholas seemed to influence the leaders of the empire, many in Myra began to think he was the most powerful person in the world. This belief was reinforced when the small cleric again found a way to stop death in its tracks.

In 333 Nicholas and the church had their hands full. Crops had failed and a famine had swept the land. Thousands were dying of starvation. As scores flocked to churches to pray, the bishop opted to employ more direct and assertive action. While he knew that the local government and even area shops had no food, he realized that several cargo ships that had just sailed into Myra were filled with wheat bound for Alexandria. Nicholas approached the captain of the convoy and asked if the man could give just a tenth of the stores to help feed the starving people of Myra. The sailor explained that if the full measure of grain did not arrive at its destination, he and his men would be punished. They could not take that risk.

Refusing to give up, Nicholas prayed with the man, shared the story of the miracle of the fishes and loaves, and then made a promise. "Give us a portion of your wheat, and I promise you in God's name that your total volume of cargo will not be lessened or diminished when you get to your destination."

The captain had to wonder what kind of magic the little man had at his beck and call. After all, wheat could not replenish itself. Yet Nicholas assured him that indeed God would protect him and his men while providing the people of Alexandria with grain. Taking a huge leap of faith, the seaman gave up more than ten percent of his cargo. Sure that he was bound for prison, he then made the journey to Egypt, only to discover that his grain weighed the same as it had when it was first loaded. None was missing.

Meanwhile, back in Myra, Nicholas set up a wheat distribution system. Though thousands came each day for their rations, the small amount taken from the ships carried the people through two years of famine, running out only after the first new crops in years were being harvested.

When the teenage Nicholas gave his inheritance to the poor, he no doubt believed he would never again have access to wealth. Yet as a bishop, he often found church coffers filled with Roman coins. While many other church leaders of the day used the funds to provide a lavish lifestyle for themselves, building great homes and purchasing the finest foods, wines, and clothing, Nicholas opted to give the money away.

As he traveled through his district, he often dropped coins into the windows of the poorest people. At times he put money in shoes that had been left on stoops and porches. Though his staff knew it was the bishop distributing these gifts, Nicholas did not allow the information to reach the public. Thus when someone rushed up to him with the news of finding a gold coin in their home, the bishop smiled and assured them that God had heard their prayers and answered their needs.

Beyond his secret gifts, Nicholas often appeared in the poorest areas of small villages, inquiring of local officials where he could find those in the greatest need. He traveled to those areas and without announcing his identity gave away money, food, and clothing, then disappeared before the shocked men and women could thank him. Most had no idea he was a clergyman, and a legend grew that he was an angel dressed in red.

As he grew older, Nicholas expanded his work to include the elderly. Thanks to his position, he was allowed to live out his final years in dignity with all his needs being met by those around him. Uncomfortable with the attention lavished on him, Nicholas pointed out to his staff that every older person in his region needed to have this same security and be shown equal compassion. So when families did not care for the elderly, he made sure the church did.

Yet what ultimately made him a legend was not his power over government or his ministry to the poor. It was his love of children that so endeared the little man to his flock. As he grew older, he used more and more of his funds to purchase gifts for children. He never went out without toys or candy. Giving them to the little ones, Nicholas told stories of Christ and the gift he had given through his death on the cross. As they attempted to understand what that meant to their lives, he added, "Jesus loves little children and he loves you." Many began to first understand the full measure of their salvation through the gifts Nicholas handed out each day.

As a servant of God, he saw himself as a shepherd to a flock of needy and often lost sheep. In that role he gave his life, being their voice in a world that seemed to care little about them. As he won his battles for the poor, as he convinced the most powerful leaders of the day to help him meet their needs and show compassion on their circumstances, he became a legend of faith. His acts of service were so great that when he died, others picked up where he left off. In fact, within just a few years children all over Myra found gifts left in their shoes on Nicholas's birthday.

Over time the legend of Nicholas of Myra grew to almost mythical proportions. He was especially revered by seamen, shopkeepers, and children. Early Christians held him in such awe that hundreds of churches were christened with his name. Yet all of this pales in light of what his compassionate life has come to mean to countless souls each Christmas.

Saint Nicholas didn't become Santa Claus by chance. Those who first provided the holidays with a magical elf dressed in red did so as a tribute to the giving spirit of this extraordinary man. Surely, if he could watch the joy on the faces of those all over the globe at Christmastime, he would be pleased that his lessons of giving are still being taught and that children everywhere are made to feel especially loved on the day that celebrates Christ's birth. As a rich man's son, Nicholas spent his life giving away everything given to him. And that giving continues to this day.

15

ALBERT SCHWEITZER
Serving a Higher Calling

On February 16, 1919, in a church in Strasbourg, France, a forty-five-year-old minister turned doctor stood before a large congregation. It was a monumental day for Albert Schweitzer. After spending time in an internment camp, he was again a free man. Yet his freedom had come at a terrible price. His hospital in Lambarene, Africa, had been destroyed. The work he had spent five years building was gone.

Looking out at the congregation, Schweitzer knew that with all he had lost, he should have felt as defeated as the kaiser's army. Yet as he stood behind the pulpit, there was again life and energy in his body. Glancing down at his well-worn Bible, he read Mark 12:28–34. He then asked the question they had posed to Jesus. "What is the greatest commandment?" As a captivated audience studied him, he launched into a message that showed people's need to hold all of life in the greatest of reverence.

"Our culture divides people into two classes: civilized men, a title bestowed on the persons who do the classifying; and others, who have only the human form, who may perish or go to the dogs for all the 'civilized men' care.

"Oh, this 'noble' culture of ours! It speaks so piously of human dignity and human rights and then disregards this dignity and these rights of countless millions and treads them underfoot, only because they live overseas or because their skins are of different color or because they cannot help themselves. This culture does not know how hollow and miserable and full of glib talk it is, how common it looks to those who follow it across the seas and see what it has done there, and this culture has no right to speak of personal dignity and human rights. . . .

"I will not enumerate all the crimes that have been committed under the pretext of justice. People robbed native inhabitants of their land, made slaves of them, let loose the scum of mankind upon them. Think of the atrocities that were perpetrated upon people made subservient to us, how systematically we have ruined them with our alcoholic gifts, and everything else we have done. . . . We decimate them, and then, by the stroke of a pen, we take their land so they have nothing left at all. . . .

"If all this oppression and all this sin and shame are perpetrated under the eye of the German God, or the American God, or the British God, and if our states do not feel obliged first to lay aside their claim to be 'Christian' — then the name of Jesus is blasphemed and made a mockery. And the Christianity of our states is blasphemed and made a mockery before those poor people. The name of Jesus has become a curse, and our Christianity — yours and mine — has become a falsehood and a disgrace, if the crimes are not atoned for in the very place where they were instigated. For every person who committed an atrocity in Jesus' name, someone must step in to help in Jesus' name; for every person who robbed, someone must bring a replacement; for everyone who cursed, someone must bless.

"And now, when you speak about missions, let this be your message: We must make atonement for all the terrible crimes we read of in the newspapers. We must make atonement for the still worse ones, which we do not read about in the papers, crimes that are shrouded in the silence of the jungle night."

He later added what would be his mantra, "If a man loses his reverence for any part of life, he will lose his reverence for all of life."

Schweitzer's words were powerful then but seem even more powerful now. Yet how he arrived at his understanding and even how he received the chance to speak on that February day explains a great deal about why he sacrificed so much of his life to live the words he so forcefully spoke on that day in 1919.

Schweitzer was born in Kaisersberg, Germany, in 1875. The son of a Lutheran minister, Schweitzer was raised in the middle of fabled wine country that had been a part of the area between Germany and France for centuries. A curious child, he carefully read the Bible and then, rather than just accepting the stories, asked questions of his father. One was, "If the men from the East gave such wonderful gifts, then what did Mary and Joseph do with the treasure? The Bible says they were poor, so what happened?"

When he wasn't studying theology, Schweitzer took long walks in the woods and field outside his village. Nature fascinated him. He found wonder in every facet of life. He could watch birds fly for hours. He often studied the differences in trees and flowers. He loved to watch deer run or even a worm crawl. For reasons he did not comprehend, each of these scenes brought him great happiness. Yet when he observed people mistreating animals, that happiness gave way to an inner rage. Tears of anger and sadness rushed to his eyes when he witnessed an old horse being whipped by a farmer or a bird shot by a hunter. These images of humankind's cruelty to animals haunted him so much that his prayers included not just his family and friends but also "all things that have breath."

On an Easter Sunday when he was nine, a close friend suggested they take their slingshots up into the mountains to hunt birds. This outing across green meadows would have a dramatic impact on the young Schweitzer. As he later described it, the excitement of the hunt quickly paled when he was confronted with the reality of the kill.

"We got close to a tree which was still without any leaves, and on which the birds were singing beautifully to greet the morning, without showing the least fear of us. Then stooping like a red Indian hunter, my companion put a bullet in the leather of his catapult and took aim. In obedience to his nod of command, I did the same, though with terrible twinges of conscience, vowing to myself that I would shoot directly [when] he did. At that very moment the church bells began to ring, mingling their music with the songs of the birds and the sunshine. It was the warning-bell which began half an hour before the regular peal-ringing, and for me it was a voice from heaven. I shooed the birds away, so that they flew where they were safe from my companion's catapult, and then I fled home. And ever since then, when the passion-tide bells ring out to the leafless trees and the sunshine, I reflect with a rush of grateful emotion, how on that day their music drove deep into my heart the commandment: Thou shall not kill."

Schweitzer would not kill from that day forward. He would never intentionally take another life or harm another creature. He had changed into a person few in this village could understand. Yet the fact that he was different did not faze the boy. Instead it pushed him to convert others to his unique view of the world.

Not far from Schweitzer's home stood a statue created by Frederic Bartholdi, the artist who gave the world the Statue of Liberty. In this work of stone a black man seemed to be carrying the weight of the world on his shoulders. The sad look etched into his face horrified Schweitzer. He was drawn to it like a magnet, trying as best he could to understand what had caused such pain. Did he, even as a boy, share in the guilt? He simply could not forget the sculpture; the image of the suffering African followed him everywhere, even into his dreams at night.

Schweitzer sought wisdom as most children seek mischief, with a passion that knew no bounds. As he studied history, he became fascinated by stories of Africa. Yet while the tales of strange wild beasts and incredible jungles naturally enthralled him, another element of his studies appalled the young student. When he read between the lines, he saw horror where his classmates saw adventure. Schweitzer realized that Europeans had raped the continent. They had stolen Africa's resources, enslaved many of its peoples, and shown no respect for the cultures that had been established for thousands of years. To his great dismay, it seemed most whites looked at Africa as nothing more than a place to claim booty. He was horrified to discover that many of his classmates saw black men and women as little more than animals. Some even said these people didn't have a soul. These views kept the child awake at night. How could people who claimed Jesus as their Savior feel this way?

Beyond possessing the ability to think and reason, Schweitzer was also gifted as a musician. By his early teens he was recognized as the foremost master of the organ in the region. It was a gift he came by naturally, as his father and grandfathers had been talented performers. As people listened to him play, many believed that Schweitzer would find both fame and fortune at the organ.

His concerts made him the nineteenth-century equivalent of a local rock star. The young ladies flocked to his side, desperate to find ways to gain this handsome man's attention. Yet at the very moment he should have been relishing his youth and the notice his talents brought his way, the image of man's inhumanity to man consumed much of his thought. So he often avoided the crowds rather than basking in his own fame.

As a college student, he made a solitary climb to the top of a mountain to contemplate what he could do to right the wrongs that had been done by centuries of people claiming to be Christian. His conclusions always led him to the same thought. He was lucky, he was blessed, and he was called, but for what? He was just twenty-one when he decided upon a plan for the remainder of his life. He didn't yet know his final destination, but he now at least had mapped out a timetable for this journey of discovery. He had the faith to believe that God would give him the means and the answers he needed before he came to that final crossroads.

"I decided that I would consider myself justified in living till I was thirty for science and art, and from that time on would devote myself to the direct service of humanity. I had often tried to settle what meaning lay hidden for me in the saying of Jesus, 'Whosoever would save his life shall lose it, and whosoever shall lose his life for my sake and the Gospel's shall save it!' Now the answer was found. In addition to the outward, I now had inward happiness."

In 1899 Schweitzer earned a doctorate in philosophy from the University of Strasbourg and immediately began preaching at the St. Nicholas Church. Not satisfied to do just a single job, he also played scores of organ concerts, wrote the defining treatise on Bach and his music, developed new methods of organ construction, and completed a book, *The Quest for the Historical Jesus*, that would become one of the most revolutionary theological works of its day. In his spare time he presided over and taught classes at a seminary, read several books a week, and wrote music. All this was in preparation for his thirtieth birthday, when he vowed he would fulfill his destiny. Yet in 1904, as that day loomed in the very near future, he still had not found what he considered his true calling.

Schweitzer's frustration with what he perceived as an unfocused life seemed bizarre. Few if any twenty-nine-year-old men had accomplished as much as he had. His books were popular all over the world. His abilities as a musician left even music masters in awe. His sermons were so well conceived that seminary students everywhere studied them. Yet in spite of all his fame and accomplishments, he was restless and depressed. He felt he was a failure because he had not been able to seize on a singular direction for his life's work, nor had he found a way to right the wrongs created by generations of human greed.

Successful but unfulfilled, in 1904 Schweitzer picked up a magazine with a feature that focused on a missionary's work in the Congo. The story's subject appealed not only for money to support his work but also for help. He begged others to come to Africa and give direct aid to poor, hungry, sick people. As Schweitzer considered what this man had sacrificed in his mission, he once again reflected on the statue near his boyhood home. For days the image of the sculpture and the plight of the Dark Continent consumed his thoughts. Like a cloud, it followed him everywhere.

During this period of angst he wrote a close friend, "Who can describe the injustice and cruelties that in the course of centuries they [African people] have suffered at the hands of Europeans. If a record could be compiled of all that has happened between the white and the colored races, it would make a book containing numbers of pages which the reader would have to turn over unread because their contents would be too horrible."

One morning he realized that if God could speak through a burning bush, he could also use the statue to guide Schweitzer. That piece of stone seemed placed in his hometown to give him the answer to where he was to spend the remainder of his life. The calling had always been there, but only now could he understand it.

In a matter of days after reading the missionary's report, Schweitzer's passion had risen to such a level that he wanted to instantly board a boat to the Congo. Yet as he looked at the needs of the African people and then examined his own experience, he realized he was woefully short in the skills needed in the jungle. He was a preacher, teacher, writer, and musician, and none of those things were of much use to illiterate people suffering from hunger and disease. So as much as he wanted to go to Africa and begin righting the wrongs of hundreds of years of European abuse, he knew he was not equipped for the job.

Faith is a strange commodity. Men and women who have a bit of faith can accomplish things others think impossible. Those blessed with faith can also endure hardship and struggle when people without it give up. In an effort to live the call he felt, a faith-filled Schweitzer gave up his jobs as teacher, preacher, writer, and musician and entered medical school. Except for one pen pal, he shared the reasons for his dramatic career change with no one.

Helene Bresslau was the daughter of a Strasbourg University history teacher. Four years younger than Schweitzer, she was well educated, energetic, and eager to challenge the world's perceptions of what a woman could do. She worked with orphans, founded a home for unmarried mothers, played organ, and was a skilled athlete. In other words, she was an emancipated woman at a time when few young women graduated high school. Her independence and drive frightened most men, but not Schweitzer. He was fascinated by her intelligence, determination, and courage. When he could not visit with her in person, he wrote long, detailed letters explaining his joys, sadness, confusion, and goals.

Initially Helene was awed by Schweitzer's drive and talent, but as the two grew closer, she became concerned over Albert's desire to work in a dangerous land where few white men and almost no white women had ventured. Helene might have been a revolutionary thinker and a woman who fought to be recognized as an equal to men, but she also wanted a home, a family, and the semblance of a normal life. After seven years in school, as Schweitzer finished his degree still intent on giving up everything to build a new life in the Congo, Helene decided that love should triumph over personal desires. Together they would live out his calling.

Schweitzer's family was shocked when he announced he was taking his bride to Africa. Friends and family argued that he would do much more good if he simply took the money from his medical practice, sales of his books, and organ concerts and sent those funds as gifts to others already doing the Lord's work in the Congo. Completely sure of his call, Schweitzer announced that it was time for action and that he could really only serve God by giving up everything to heal the wounds created by generations of uncaring Christians. Yet even his strong faith ran into a huge obstacle.

Schweitzer possessed a world of knowledge and a heart filled with passion but had spent all of his money. He had no financial foundation for the medical practice he had vowed to create. Thus the trip was delayed as he played a series of farewell organ concerts to generate funds needed to buy medicines, equipment, and supplies. The adulation he received during these performances would have turned a lesser man's head. Fans wanted his autograph, bookers pleaded with him to extend his tour and play in America and Asia, and record companies begged him to put his talent on wax. Yet when he reached the goal needed to fund his mission, Schweitzer quit. At thirty-eight he declared it was time to give his life fully to God.

On Good Friday 1913, Albert and Helene Schweitzer, who were then German citizens, boarded a ship headed for a French colony in Africa. Neither had been there before, they had no idea what to expect, and yet their faith was so strong that they did not show any fear to those who had come to see them off.

The journey was plagued by stormy weather. When they arrived off the coast of Gabon, they were worn out. Yet the trip was far from over; now the couple had to board a small boat to take them up the Ogowe River to a tiny outpost known as Lambarene.

As he sat in the tiny vessel, the new doctor's first impressions of Africa were overwhelming. It was even more exotic, amazing, and terrifying than he had imagined. He had never seen so many different kinds of animals and flora. He had never felt such heat, never dreamed that there could be this much humidity without rain. Even with his training in medicine, was he equipped to handle the challenge that now filled his eyes and senses? He was but one man in a world that seemed astonishingly large.

"We seemed to be dreaming," Schweitzer later wrote of his first trip to what became his home. "It is impossible to say where the river ends and the land begins. White birds and blue birds skim over the water, and high in the air a pair of ospreys circle. Then—yes; there can be no mistake about it—from the branch of a palm there hang and swing—two monkey tails! Now the owners of the tails are visible. We are really in Africa!"

The couple's destination was an established missionary outpost where they had been promised a piece of ground and a small house.

Schweitzer had assumed that he would be given at least half a year to set up his facilities and then begin seeing patients. Yet for months the news that a European doctor was coming to Lambarene had spread through the jungle. The word went out: "Bring your sick, he is coming!"

As he pulled up to the dock, an exhausted and overwhelmed Schweitzer was greeted by hundreds of men, women, and children, many of whom had been waiting for days. Many had traveled hundreds of miles, enduring hunger, rain, and scorching heat just to see him. Some were so ill, they were closer to death than life. They could not wait for the doctor to set up a practice; their needs had to be met now.

Thus, out in the open, with only a table and a chair, the doctor and his wife went to work. For weeks of sixteen-hour days, they treated patients under the unrelenting sun and even in the midst of thunderstorms. Finally, sensing they had to have at least a semblance of a real office, they scared a flock of birds out of a chicken coop and called it a clinic. For months this was all there was to Schweitzer's missionary hospital.

Over the next two years, the couple worked ten hours a day treating patients and another six to eight hours a day constructing buildings. In time the riverbank began to resemble a crude medical facility. It was not what Schweitzer had envisioned, but for what he needed to do, it served his purposes. Then, just when everything began to mesh, just when support from Europe and America began to reach his work and volunteers began arriving to help, World War I broke out. Even though the real battles were a continent away, Schweitzer found himself in the middle of a fight to the death.

As German citizens, the Schweitzers were seen as enemies of those in the French-controlled Congo. At first they were placed under house arrest and allowed to treat patients. Yet as the conflict grew into a worldwide war, the couple was moved to an internment camp in France. In this prisonlike facility, a pregnant Helene developed tuberculosis, and the doctor learned his mother had died in the fighting. Even for a man like Schweitzer, with death all around him, suddenly faith was in short supply.

World War I was like nothing Schweitzer had ever imagined. On a daily basis he saw the effects of modern weaponry, of nerve gas, of mustard gas, and of the rage of men fighting each other. As he studied the joy many seemed to gain from inflicting pain and suffering, he began to question the value of the human race. Was it worth saving? Would the world be better if humankind were wiped out? His observation as a Christian was summed up with his view that "we can do all things, and we can do nothing, for in all our wisdom we are not able to create life. Rather, what we create is death."

The fatalistic view of a modern world, contrasted with the love and acceptance he had found in Africa, helped Schweitzer create his philosophy of reverence for life. He believed that all life is sacred and that he should do no harm to either another person or any of God's creatures. This idea that started in a prison camp would continue to form as he, his wife, and their new daughter were released back to a Europe that had seen more death and destruction in just two years than it had in the last ten centuries.

Now free, the Schweitzers were not just broke; they were up to their ears in debt. The mission they had worked day and night for years to build had been destroyed, and the bridge back to that place seemed impossible to reconstruct. They owed bills for medicines and supplies ordered for an African hospital that no longer existed. So now they had no idea what they would do or where they would go.

In a very real sense, the light that had caused the Schweitzers to give up everything to go to the Congo burned no more. It might never have been relit if they had not received an invitation from an old friend.

Nathan Soderblom, archbishop of Sweden, asked Schweitzer to lecture at the University of Uppsala and used his contacts to gain speaking engagements for Schweitzer. Soderblom also promised a salary and a place for the Schweitzers to live. Suddenly there was hope again. In fact, this experience later led the doctor to explain how he maintained his faith in tough times. "At times our own light goes out; it is rekindled by a spark from another person. Each of us has cause to think with deep gratitude of those who have lighted the flame within us." In this case Soderblom not only relit the flame; he found ways for the missionary doctor to make the money he needed to pay off his debts and return to Africa.

The archbishop used his connections to organize a lecture tour, then opened the door for organ concerts, and finally helped find a publisher for Schweitzer's books. For six years Schweitzer used these opportunities to make money to rebuild his beloved mission. During one of these speaking engagements in Strasbourg, he gave a sermon that is still stirring souls today. More than any other message he ever delivered, the speech at St. Nicholas opened the door for the world to fully understand the wisdom and determination of this remarkable man.

In 1924, at the age of forty-nine, Schweitzer journeyed back to Africa to once more start from scratch. Within three years he had rebuilt his initial facility and added two more hospitals. This was just the beginning. Even as he treated hundreds each day, he oversaw continued construction of everything from kitchens to family shelters.

As news of his work made its way through the jungle, it also found its way around the globe. Donations began to pour in from almost every modern nation and every Christian denomination. Volunteers came for weeks and many stayed for years.

Yet all of this paled in comparison with the gratitude Schweitzer received from the African people he doctored. The white man who could have been one of the most celebrated men in Europe was helping to change the white race's perspective of Africa and its people. And yet as they tried to thank him, Schweitzer always gently smiled and replied, "It was the Lord Jesus who sent the doctor to you and the Lord Jesus who took the pain away."

For more than four decades the man who could have been wealthy was a poor doctor, pastor, village administrator, and tour guide in Lambarene. As his fame grew, so did the honors he was given. Yet he had no use for fame; he accepted the awards only because he knew they would pave the way for more donations to his work and perhaps would inspire others to treat all people with respect and love.

In 1952, when he won the Nobel Prize and was asked how he had done what he did, he smiled and pointed to something he had once told some students: "I don't know what your destiny will be, but one thing I know: the only ones among you who will be really happy are those who will have sought and found how to serve." Truly this doctor-missionary was very happy.

In 1965, when Schweitzer died after nine decades on earth, his chicken coop clinic had grown into a facility that included a fully equipped, air-conditioned operating theater, X-ray room, laboratory, dental clinic, delivery room, doctors' offices, and dispensary. Once it had been only him and his wife; now the staff included six doctors and thirty-five nurses. There were beds for six hundred patients, and almost ten thousand were treated at the facilities each year. Thousands of babies had been born at the clinic, and many were named Albert.

In his later years, working just as hard as he ever had, he once told an American visitor, "Life becomes harder for us when we live for others, but it also becomes richer and happier too." He added, "Example is not the main thing in influencing others, it's the only thing."

Yet Schweitzer's remarkable mission might never have been completed, the incredible things he accomplished might never have been realized, and many might never have been touched by his life and example if Nathan Soderblom had not reached out to him when war, death, and debt wiped out the missionary doctor's faith. One man's spark lifted Albert Schweitzer out of despair, and as a result millions experienced Jesus through the touch of the doctor's hands.

16

JIM VALVANO
Embracing Every Moment

James Thomas Anthony Valvano had been in intense pain for weeks. Though few around him realized it, the forty-six-year-old ESPN analyst and former coach was being tortured every minute. It had begun as a throbbing in his back but then grew to a point where it shot through his body like electrical pulses. It now affected everything he did, from walking to sleeping. At times the pain was so intense, he felt like hitting his head against the wall.

Yet Valvano kept going, kept working football games in Europe and various sporting events in the United States. He kept delivering motivational speeches and giving his time to charitable fundraisers. But now after months of solitary fighting, he had finally given up trying to handle this by himself. Whatever this was, it was far bigger than the legendary Jimmy V. So he was forced to seek help.

Sitting in a doctor's office, waiting on test results that might reveal the source of his pain, Jim tried to put his life into perspective. As was his nature, he thought about what had brought him to this place and time. As he often explained to others, you have to know where you have come from to appreciate where you are and have an idea as to where you are going next. For Jim there had been a lot more ups than downs, a lot more highs than lows, but memories of elements of his storybook life still caused him almost as much pain as whatever was attacking his body at this moment.

Born in 1946, Jim was the product of a close-knit Italian-American family in New York City who loved music, sports, food, and church. His father, Rocco, was a high school teacher and coach with a huge zest for life. Rocco's enthusiasm bubbled over, and naturally all three of his sons grew up with a deep love for all sports. They followed the Yankees, prayed for Joe Dimaggio and Mickey Mantle, tossed around the football in the streets in front of their modest home, and shot hoops on any indoor or outdoor basketball court they could find.

Raised during a period when the city spawned some of the greatest musical groups of the rock-and-roll era, Jim also embraced music. He loved to sing; there was a joy in music that seemed to lift his soul higher than even the city's tallest skyscraper. And though he would never have been confused for a member of the great local group Dion and the Belmonts or the Italian icon Frank Sinatra, he still loved to charm those around him with his voice. In fact, charm was one thing that Jim had in spades.

As he grew into his teens, Jim developed street smarts, and he could adapt to any situation and any group. He had friends from all of the city's ethnic groups, could speak to people of all ages, and was just as at home visiting with nuns as with the garbagemen who worked his streets. He saw himself as above none of them and a part of all of them. This quality made him unique and paved the way for great success in two high-profile professions.

Yet beyond his street smarts, Jim was just as curious about what could be found in books. He loved to read and was drawn to everything from the greats in American literature to biographies of men such as Albert Schweitzer and Vince Lombardi. At an early age he realized that each person he met and each thing he read changed him a bit. The growth that came through his studies fueled a passion to make a big and lasting statement with his own life. So while he loved his youth in Long Island and thrived at Seaford High School, he also wanted to make a mark on a much broader plane.

Over time, as Jim himself became a great high school athlete, he saw where two elements of Schweitzer's and Lombardi's lives came together. Though they were very different in their choice of careers, both were goal oriented, both wrote their dreams down on paper, and both put in motion a plan to make those dreams a reality. So at a time when most young men could barely decide what to do that day, Jim was sketching out a road map for his entire life on a white index card.

With great certainty he wrote that he would play basketball in college, follow that by becoming an assistant basketball coach, and finally become a head coach. He would someday return to his hometown and win a game in Madison Square Garden. He would also coach a college team to a national championship. Then he would move on to the NBA and lead the New York Knicks to a title. By accomplishing those things, Jim was sure he would make his mark.

Many kids dream big dreams, but few achieve them. For scores the missing ingredient is not talent but faith. Jim was fortunate because his father gave him the greatest gift a father could give a son. Rocco constantly told the boy, "I believe you can do it, son." At eighteen years old, Jim already possessed a father's faith and his hand-scrawled goal card, and they seemed to be all he needed.

Jim got a scholarship to Rutgers University. With Jim directing the traffic from his point guard position, the Scarlet Knights finished third in the 1967 National Invitational Tournament. The last game the team won was at Madison Square Garden. That same year Jim was named Athlete of the Year at Rutgers and graduated with a degree in English. Now married to his high school sweetheart, Pamela Levine, the gangly young man with the toothy grin was on his way to making his mark. He was already scratching out accomplishments on his list.

After a stint as an assistant coach at Rutgers, Jim was named the head basketball coach at Johns Hopkins before moving to Bucknell and finally landing at Iowa. With his huge smile, his great ability to spin a story, and his natural charisma, he was a success at each stop. Yet in order for him to have a shot at an NCAA title, he knew he would have to win an opportunity to coach in one of the nation's elite conferences. That chance came when the president of North Carolina State University asked permission to visit with Jim.

Showing the young New Yorker around the campus, the athletic director told him, "We're naming our coach tomorrow. Do you want the job?" Shocked, Jim asked about the salary and length of the contract. The answer he received was at best cryptic. "We will work that out later. Do you want the job?"

Jim's family was growing; he had a good financial deal and a long contract at Iowa. Now if he took the North Carolina State job, he would be walking into something with no guarantees. Beyond that, this was North Carolina, where basketball was more than a passion — it was almost a religion. Even though State had won a national title in 1974, the Wolfpack basketball program was down, which is why the school was looking for a new coach. Nothing short of another national championship would satisfy the administration or the fans.

The odds against his having that kind of success were long. Yet in Jim's pocket was a card. That card clearly spelled out the need to be at a program like State's to achieve his next goal. Now did he have the faith to make that step?

The key to Jim's decision was his father's belief in him. Rocco truly felt that his son could win as coach of the Wolfpack, and he assured him of that. So with the support of the man whose trust he treasured, Jim took the leap of faith while praying it was the right thing to do.

From his first days of coaching, Jim had always told his team, "Everyday, ordinary people can do extraordinary things." Now the city-bred, street-smart coach had to convince the kids on Tobacco Road they could compete with the giants in basketball.

From day one he asked his players to write down their goals. He wanted to know how large their dreams were and how much they were willing to sacrifice to achieve them. He told them about the work ethic of men like Schweitzer and Lombardi. Just as those two legends had explained to their teams, he explained that the individuals who made up NC State had to become a unit and bury themselves in that unit. Like a Southern evangelist he preached, "You must dream and you must work, and if you do, then you can believe you can do the impossible."

In his first two years Jim recruited kids who bought into that philosophy. He daily told his players they had greatness locked inside them; they just had to work hard enough and believe deeply enough to bring it out. And he gave them something his father had given him. He assured them he believed in them even more than they believed in themselves.

In 1983, just three years after taking over as coach, Jim had the North Carolina State fans excited. The team rushed out to an incredible start, but then, due to an injury to a star player, at the midpoint of the season they seemed to collapse. By the time the ACC tourney rolled around, the team was off the radar and not expected to make the NCAA tournament. Yet using all the motivational stories he knew, Jim took over. He produced a plan, sold his kids on that plan, and then, through coaching brilliance, pulled them through a series of upsets.

Picked to be knocked out in the first round of the ACC and NCAA tournaments, Jim found magic. In come-from-behind wins he got buckets from kids who rarely played, and in the midst of March Madness found his team playing for the national title against a Houston squad that already had been crowned as one of the greatest college units to ever take the court.

Jim sold his kids on the David and Goliath story. During a critical part of the game, when one of his worst free-throw shooters was fouled, Jim spent an entire time-out explaining to the young man that this moment in time was the reason Jim had recruited him. He then clarified his faith in the teenager. "I knew when I signed you to play for us, you would be in this position, and I know you'll make the shots."

The young man did make those key charity tosses. And a few minutes later, in a play that is still shown countless times each year, Dereck Whittenburg tossed up a hopeless air ball that was rebounded by Lorenzo Charles. Without coming down, Charles dunked the ball as time expired. Houston had won twenty-six straight games until that last-second shot took the wind out of their sails. The team that featured three future Basketball Hall of Famers was forced to watch as the Wolfpack faithful went wild. If not the most exciting championship game ever played, it was certainly the one with the most unexpected result. Except for those who had listened to Jim, no one had predicted this outcome. David had beaten the giant!

In the chaotic moments after the final bell, Jim rushed around the court trying to locate someone to hug. He needed someone to share the moment, because to him solitary joy was meaningless. Life had to be shared. Yet his players were all locked in each other's arms, and as he dashed through the maze of celebrating fans, the coach couldn't find anyone to share an embrace. This was a moment he had planned twenty years before, and now he didn't know what to do with it.

That moment of searching gave fans a real glimpse into Jim's soul. Above everything else, he needed people. He had to have them around him. He had to make them laugh. He had to inspire them. He had to share with them not just his stories but also what he had learned from his life. Without people he was simply lost. He lived to be a part of a family. It was everything to him. Yet, as he would find out, earthly success can be temporal, and those who embrace you at the top often disappear when times get dark and storms appear on the horizon.

During a decade as Jim was head coach at NC State, his teams were the ACC tournament champions and regular-season champions twice. They also had success on a national level, going to the

Elite 8 in 1985 and 1986. Twice voted ACC Coach of the Year, Jim was even given the additional duties of athletic director in 1986.

Then came the nightmare that was 1989. The brash man who had been in the center of every spotlight suddenly found himself completely alone. In one moment the winner had become the loser.

In a book called *Personal Fouls*, author Peter Golenbock accused Jim of a long list of NCAA rule violations. Golenbock basically labeled the North Carolina State coach a cheater. Quickly tried in the press, Jim was found guilty before he or the NCAA could even respond. Newspapers called for his ouster. Fans cried that Jimmy V. stood for all the things that were wrong with college sports. Stripped of his post as athletic director, Jim kept coaching, but even the ever optimistic Valvano knew his days at State were numbered.

Six groups investigated the basketball program, including the Faculty Senate, the North Carolina Attorney General, the University of North Carolina Board of Governors, the NC State Board of Trustees, and the NCAA. The unanimous verdicts of those separate investigations found no academic, recruiting, or financial improprieties. Yet though those reports clearly showed the coach knew nothing about the minor violations of players selling shoes and tickets, the North Carolina State administration pushed Jim out. Thanks to *Personal Fouls* and the actions taken by his school, the coach who had been known as the miracle worker was now viewed by most Americans as a criminal. He couldn't even find a job teaching at a junior high school.

Deeply wounded, Jim retreated to his home, spending time with his wife, Pamela, and their three daughters, Nicole, Jamie, and Lee Ann. The future looked bleak. Essentially, there was no way for him to make a living and no forum in which he could prove his innocence. At the age of forty-four it was as if he were dead.

Jimmy drew a bit of solace from a letter written by the lead NCAA investigator in the case, saying he would be proud to have his son play for the coach. Yet this tribute was tempered by the fact that Jim knew he was never going to be given the chance to coach again. For all practical purposes, his life in basketball and in the spotlight seemed over. The toothy grin and the bouncy walk were lost forever. The man who once made everyone he met feel as though they mattered wondered if he would ever matter again. Yet even when the world had given up on the coach, it seemed God had other plans.

In 1992 ABC needed a color analyst for their expanded coverage of college basketball. The head of sports for ABC/ESPN was Dennis Swanson. When one of Jim's friends pitched the former coach for the new job, the network's team of advisors all shook their heads. They considered the former coach toxic. Yet that didn't keep Swanson from calling those who knew Jim well and asking about the man's character. Swayed by the words of several top coaches, he scheduled a visit. This would be a meeting both would never forget. In the span of just a few minutes Swanson decided the disgraced coach was worth a second chance.

One of Jim's favorite quote's came from Albert Schweitzer. He had shared the missionary doctor's words many times with others going through tough times. Now the former coach could apply them to his own life. Schweitzer had said, "At times our own light goes out; it is rekindled by a spark from another person. Each of us has cause to think with deep gratitude of those who have lighted the flame within us." Swanson and the friends who had come to bat for Jim had relit his faith. He called each of them to personally thank them for bringing that spark back into his world.

What he had been through since losing his job at NC State had caused Jim to realize that he was not really in control of his destiny. The goals on the index card were nice, they gave him direction and focus, but it was God who was in control. So now, more than at any time during his coaching career, Jim decided that he needed to share his faith with others. After a lifetime of letting the world see his brash and almost arrogant confidence, it was now time for the world to see his faith.

Jim was a natural on TV. He was so good that ABC took him beyond basketball and allowed him to cover almost all of their major sporting events. The smile and wit that had made him a great recruiter and fundraiser as a coach now won him even more friends. Surveys found he was popular with viewers because they saw something in him they didn't see in others. His tone and words clearly showed he was not just doing a job; he cared about the people he was covering and those who were listening.

Because of this attitude, doors opened up like they never had before. When he wasn't covering sports for ABC, he was giving motivational speeches to corporations, hosting a radio show, or doing guest appearances on *The Tonight Show*, *David Letterman*, and even *The Cosby Show*. He was living as if every day were a gift and constantly trying to share that attitude with others. And now that journey, begun on the streets of New York City, had taken him to a doctor's office.

The doctor was obviously nervous as he came into the room. After trying to smile, he grimly told Jim, "You have metastatic adenocarcinoma—that's a bone cancer, in layman's terms. It has spread all over your body, and I'm afraid there is nothing we can do. I wish I could give you better news, but you probably have less than a year to live."

Jim nodded, slowly got up, and shook the doctor's hand. After thanking the physician for his time, he walked slowly to his car. Yet even now, at the very worst moment of his life, Jim could still hear his late father saying, "I believe in you, son. I have faith in you, Jim."

Jimmy V. was now acutely aware that there were 86,400 seconds in each day. How many did he have left, and what could he do with them? With the clock ticking and every painful breath bringing him closer to life's final buzzer, Jim decided not to wait for death at home. He would go back to work.

As news got out about his illness, the letters started to pour in. Friends, players, old coaches, and fans wrote to him by the thousands. Many told him they were praying for him, others offered hopes for new treatments, and a few explained how his smile and upbeat words had inspired them to face their own problems. In those letters, Jim discovered he had the potential to be an even greater light than he had been as a coach. Maybe he could change the outcome of the game and create another comeback victory!

When people wrote him, he took the time to offer them a chance to join his team. He even sent them a card to carry that said,

> I am a member of Valvano's Incredible Cancer Team of Really Important Extraordinary Stars.
> Every day I will:
>
> Say to myself, "Jimmy V., you will make it."
> Say out loud, "Jimmy V., hang in there."
> Ask God to help Jimmy V.
> Do something to strengthen myself mentally, physically, and spiritually.
>
> Welcome to the Team!

Jim sent out his cards by the thousands, and many of those who got them took them to heart. They did start praying more, reading the Bible, and even exercising. As he received follow-up reports from the members of his new team, Jim decided to become cancer's poster child. He would put the disease front and center and try to find a game plan to coach himself and others to victory.

Invited back to North Carolina State to help celebrate the tenth anniversary of the national championship, he brought the crowd to its feet as he took the microphone. Just three years after he was forced out, he was again in the spotlight.

"Let me tell you what the '83 team means to me," he began. "They're special not because they put that banner up there. They're special because they taught me and the world so many important lessons.

"Number 1: Hope. What does hope mean, hope that things can get better in spite of adversity?

"The '83 team taught me about dreaming and the importance of dreams, because nothing can happen if not first a dream. If you have someone with a dream, you have a motivated person with a dream and a goal and a vision.

"When you have a goal, when you have a dream, and when you have a belief, and you throw in that concept of never stop believing in and loving each other, you can accomplish miracles.

"Today I fight a different battle. You see I have trouble walking. And I have trouble standing for long periods of time. Cancer has taken away a lot of my physical abilities. But I have faith in God and in my fellow man that things might get better for me. And I have tremendous love for all of the people who care about me and my family. It's because I know what hope and what faith and what belief and what hard work and good people can do. I will never give up my fight.

"And if by chance the Lord wants me, he's going to get the best broadcaster and ex-basketball coach that they've ever had up there. Thank you and God bless you, everybody."

After his speech scores of people from his former school called and asked how they could give to help him fight cancer. Could the North Carolina State speech, which many had seen as a dying man's farewell bow, be a springboard for something greater? Could Jim find a way to take his last game into overtime?

Because of Jim's uplifting attitude, everyone from the janitors to cameramen to anchors and producers were now wrapped up in the former coach's fight. Sensing ESPN had become a second family to Jim, Dennis Swanson opted to get involved in helping fund a grassroots campaign that had been created by Jim's cards and speeches. Swanson met with his broadcaster to get a feel for his goals, and the two men quickly put together the Jimmy V. Foundation. Its sole purpose would be to raise funds for cancer research.

Now realizing there would be no miracle for his case, Jim prayed he could live long enough to somehow kick-start the foundation's work. Suddenly nothing else mattered, not the goals he had accomplished, not the national championship, and certainly not the awards. Those were human things, and they had no real lasting impact. Jim had to do something that would become God's work. Was it too late? Did a dying man still have the time to light a fire of enthusiasm and faith?

With the clock now ticking faster, with each step now coming more slowly and the pain growing in intensity, Jim pushed himself to work even harder. There was no comfortable position for him to sit or stand in, yet he refused most pain medications because he needed to stay mentally aware. He was constantly and desperately searching for a spotlight. He had so much to say and so little time left to say it.

At the same time that Jim was told he had cancer, ESPN's marketing department realized that of all the major forms of entertainment, only sports did not have its own awards show. Thus in 1993 the network created the ESPYs. One of the awards to be given on March 3 at Madison Square Garden would be for courage. The person chosen to receive that honor was Jim Valvano.

Sick, weak, and barely able to stand, Jim flew with his wife, daughters, and a few friends from North Carolina to New York to attend the ceremony. He was a physical wreck, but he forced himself to come in order to put the spotlight on the disease that was taking his life. If his life was to stand for anything, he wanted it to be a beacon for the fight against cancer. Over the past nine months that had become his calling. Thus he viewed this moment, with millions looking on via television, as a God-given answer to a prayer.

Jim was pale and rail thin. Countless tumors were ravaging his body as he walked to the Madison Square Garden stage that night. He looked more dead than alive as he was helped to the podium to receive the award. Yet it quickly become obvious that Jim's light was still shining and that his faith was still intact. As he looked out at the audience and heard the applause, his energy and smile magically returned. He knew this was it! This was why he had fought so hard to keep going. Now was why God had placed him on earth and given him all the ups and downs and high and lows. Now, could he find the words to make a difference?

"I'm fighting cancer, everybody knows that," he said. "People ask me all the time about how you go through your life and how's your day, and nothing is changed for me. As Dick said, I'm a very emotional, passionate man. I can't help it. That's being the son of Rocco and Angelina Valvano. It comes with the territory. We hug, we kiss, we love. And when people say to me how do you get through life or each day, it's the same thing. To me, there are three things we all should do every day. We should do this every day of our lives. Number one is laugh. You should laugh every day. Number two is think. You should spend some time in thought. And number three is, you should have your emotions moved to tears, could be happiness or joy. But think about it. If you laugh, you think, and you cry, that's a full day. That's a heck of a day. You do that seven days a week, you're going to have something special.

"I urge all of you, all of you, to enjoy your life, the precious moments you have. To spend each day with some laughter and some thought, to get your emotions going. To be enthusiastic every day and [as] Ralph Waldo Emerson said, 'Nothing great could be accomplished without enthusiasm' — to keep your dreams alive in spite of problems whatever you have. [Then you have] the ability to be able to work hard for your dreams to come true, to become a reality.

"Now I look at where I am now and I know what I wanna do. What I would like to be able to do is to spend whatever time I have left and to give, and maybe some hope to others.

"We need your help. I need your help. We need money for research. It may not save my life. It may save my children's lives. It may save someone you love. And it's very important.

"We are starting the Jimmy V. Foundation for Cancer Research, and its motto is 'Don't give up, don't ever give up.' And that's what I'm going to try to do every minute that I have left. I will thank God for the day and the moment I have. And if you see me, smile and maybe give me a hug. That's important to me too. But try if you can to support, whether it's AIDS or the cancer foundation, so that someone else might survive, might prosper, and might actually be cured of this dreaded disease. I can't thank ESPN enough for allowing this to happen. And I'm going to work as hard as I can ... for cancer research and hopefully, maybe, we'll have some cures and some breakthroughs.

"I know, I gotta go, I gotta go, and I got one last thing and I said it before, and I'm gonna say it again: Cancer can take away all my physical ability. It cannot touch my mind; it cannot touch my heart; and it cannot touch my soul. And those three things are going to carry on forever.

"I thank you and God bless you all."

One of Jim's heroes, Vince Lombardi, once said, "I firmly believe that any man's finest hour, the greatest fulfillment of all that he holds dear, is that moment when he has worked his heart out in a good cause and lies exhausted on the field of battle — victorious." On this night, in his hometown, at the venue where he had always planned to win a huge game, Jimmy V. won the biggest contest of his life, and millions jumped on board to join his team.

On April 28, 1993, less than a year after being told he was terminal, and just fifty-five days after delivering what is now considered the most famous sports speech of all time, Jim Valvano died at the young age of forty-seven. Though he found his true calling only after a disease had robbed him of much of his vitality and strength, he was able to follow his calling long enough to initiate a miracle. The foundation he kick-started with his ESPY speech has now raised more than eighty million dollars. The progress made through this work has helped save tens of thousands of lives, including the life of one of his daughters. Through his final speech and his foundation, Jim's faith lives on and continues to motivate, inspire, excite, and move ordinary people to do extraordinary things. His light still shines.

Stories behind Women of Extraordinary Faith

Ace Collins, Bestselling Author

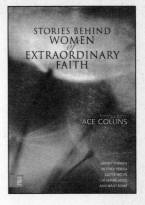

Twenty women whose faith has re-shaped the world.

Ace Collins employs all his story-telling skill to uncover the deeply personal stories of women whose faith shines for us today. Explore twenty different tales of unparalleled inspiration. Learn how each woman's prayers were heard and answered, and discover how each story can light the way on your own journey of faith.

Hardcover, Jacketed: 978-0-310-26316-6

Pick up a copy today at your favorite bookstore!

Lije Evans Mysteries

Farraday Road

Ace Collins, Bestselling Author

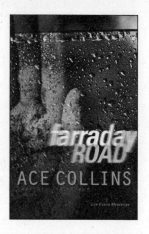

A quiet evening ends in murder on a muddy mountain road.

Local attorney Lije Evans and his beautiful wife, Kaitlyn, are gunned down. But the killers don't expect one of their victims to live. After burying Kaitlyn, Lije is on a mission to find her killer — and solve a mystery that has more twists and turns than an Ozark-mountain back road.

When the trail of evidence goes cold, complicated by the disappearance of the deputy who found Kaitlyn's body at the scene of the crime, Lije is driven to find out why he and his wife were hunted down and left for dead along Farraday Road. He begins his dangerous investigation with no clues and little help from the police. As he struggles to uncover evidence, will he learn the truth before the killers strike again?

Softcover: 978-0-310-27952-5

Pick up a copy today at your favorite bookstore!

Sticks and Stones

Using Your Words as a Positive Force

Ace Collins, Bestselling Author

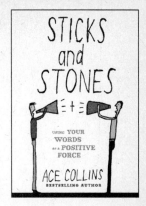

Of the roughly thirty-thousand words you will speak today, imagine if just a handful of them could save a life ... or heal a broken heart ... or inspire a vision that shapes the course of history.

Today is your opportunity to speak — or write — words of incalculable potential for good. With simple action points and colorful stories, this inspiring book will help you weed out sticks-and-stones negativism and unleash the surpassing, life-giving, destiny-shaping power of positive words.

What does it take for your words to make a difference? Perhaps a simple thank-you letter. Maybe an encouraging email. Or a simple hello, a thoughtful phone call, a note written on the back of a family photograph ... the possibilities are endless. *Sticks and Stones* shows you the power and importance of your words, and how to use the right words to have a positive impact beyond anything you can imagine.

Hardcover, Jacketed: 978-0-310-28253-2

Share Your Thoughts

With the Author: Your comments will be forwarded to the author when you send them to *zauthor@zondervan.com*.

With Zondervan: Submit your review of this book by writing to *zreview@zondervan.com*.

Free Online Resources at
www.zondervan.com

Zondervan AuthorTracker: Be notified whenever your favorite authors publish new books, go on tour, or post an update about what's happening in their lives.

Daily Bible Verses and Devotions: Enrich your life with daily Bible verses or devotions that help you start every morning focused on God.

Free Email Publications: Sign up for newsletters on fiction, Christian living, church ministry, parenting, and more.

Zondervan Bible Search: Find and compare Bible passages in a variety of translations at www.zondervanbiblesearch.com.

Other Benefits: Register yourself to receive online benefits like coupons and special offers, or to participate in research.

ZONDERVAN®
.com